POVERTY AND DEVELOPMENT

EVANGELICAL CHRISTIAN RESPONSE TO POVERTY IN THE PHILIPPINES

KUMAR ARYAL

ABBREVIATIONS

ADB Asian Development Bank

ADRA Adventist Development and Relief Agency

ALS Alternative Learning System

ASEAN Association of Southeast Asian Nations

BASECO Batangas Shipping and Engineering Company

BDAG Bauer, Danker, Arndt, Gingrich

CCF Christ's Commission Fellowship

CCT Center for Community Transformation

CDRC Citizens' Disaster Response Center

CoMSCA Community Managed Savings and Credit Association

FBO Faith-Based Organization

FGD Focus Group Discussion

FH Food for the Hungry

GCF Greenhills Christian Fellowship

GAIN Global Aid Network

IMF International Monetary Fund

IGSL International Graduate School of Leadership

INGO International Non-Governmental Organization

MDG Millennium Development Goal

NGO Non-Governmental Organization

OFW Overseas Filipino Worker

PCEC Philippine Council of Evangelical Churches

PCNC Philippine Council for NGO Certification

POEA Philippine Overseas Employment Administration

PSA Philippine Statistics Authority

SWS Social Weather Stations

UN United Nations

UNDP United Nations Development Program

ACKNOWLEDGMENTS

First of all, I would like to thank God for His grace, strength and wisdom. Without God this would not have been possible. I am grateful for my wife Kathryn for her continuous prayer and encouragement to write this book. She took care of our two handsome and active boys Kevin and Kyle while I was busy writing. I would like to extend my sincere gratitude to Dr. Reynaldo S. Taniajura, Dr. Yalin Xin, Dr. Timothy L. Undheim and Dr. Jason Richard Tan for their invaluable insights, feedback and guidance. Without their guidance and mentoring, I would not have been able to complete this book.

I am grateful for the pastors and leaders of the churches, NGOs, and INGOs for their willingness to be interviewed. Their openness to share their experiences and expertise added so much depth in this book. My sincere appreciation goes to all the brothers and sisters in Cainta, BASECO, Payatas and Novaliches who willingly participated in focus group discussions. I am also grateful to International Graduate School of Leadership for allowing me to take time-off from my roles and responsibilities to focus on this project. Last but not the least, I would like to express my heartfelt gratitude to all my friends, family and prayer partners who continually journeyed with me and prayed for me to be able to complete this book.

INTRODUCTION

Poverty is one of the major problems the world is facing today. Billions of people around the world, including evangelical Christians, are living in poverty. That could be one of the reasons why evangelical Christians have been actively involved in poverty alleviation efforts. For many, poverty is mainly an economic, material, political, social and mental issue. But, for evangelical Christians, poverty is also a spiritual issue in addition to the aforementioned aspects. Evangelical Christian involvement in poverty alleviation efforts around the world has grown rapidly in the last half century, though its roots go back to the beginning of the19[th] century. It began when American Protestant churches started sending missionaries around the world (Olsen 2016, 5), including the Philippines.

The Philippines is generally known as the largest Christian country in Asia and the fifth largest Christian country in the world (Guzman 2011). According to Pew Research Center's Religion & Public Life Project, 92.6% of the total population of the Philippines consider themselves Christians. Though it is known as a Christian country, it is predominantly Roman Catholic. "Evangelicals comprise 12.19% out of the total population of 103,742,000" (Joshua Project 2018). According to Philippine Challenge, there are 66,000 evangelical churches in the Philippines (Philippine Challenge 2018). It includes "the Philippine Council of Evangelical Churches (PCEC) which is made up of more than 30,000 congregations nationwide" (PCEC 2017).

According to the Philippine Council for NGO Certification (PCNC), "there are as many as 60,000 non-governmental organizations registered in the Philippines today" (PCNC 2017), many of which are evangelical Christian NGOs. Likewise, Grace Gorospe-Jamon and Mary Grace P. Mirandilla in their chapter, "A Look at the Philippine Experience" in the book *Whither the Philippines in the 21st Century?* argue that, as of 2007, there were over 50,000 evangelical and Protestant churches in the Philippines that were actively involved in socioeconomic arenas through its faith-based organizations (Severino and Salazar 2007, 107). Thus, there are thousands of evangelical churches, NGOs, and INGOs that are working on poverty alleviation.

I have selected Metro Manila as a case study for this book because, in spite of the visible presence of evangelical Christian churches, NGOs, and INGOs, poverty remains a critical problem in this megacity. Metro Manila is also known as the National Capital Region (NCR). According to the 2003 UN-Habitat report, *The Challenge of Slums*, in 2001, Metro Manila had 526 slum communities comprised of 2.5 million people. Today the slum population of Metro Manila is more than 4 million. Most of the slums are located on unoccupied private and government owned lands, along rivers and creeks, in garbage dumps, along railway tracks, and under bridges. Poverty is growing in major cities around the world at an alarming rate, but more so in Metro Manila (Wanak 2008, 228).

According to the National Statistics Authority, 21.6 million people were living below the poverty line based on the total population of 100.98 million in August 2015. A minimum income of 9140 pesos per month required to meet basic food and nonfood needs constitutes the poverty line (Bersales 2017). The proportion of households living below the poverty line has declined very slowly and unevenly in the past four decades. It has been much slower in the Philippines than in neighboring countries such as Vietnam, Thailand, Indonesia and Cambodia (ADB 2018).

It is alarming that about one-fifth of the population in the Philippines is still living under the poverty line. However, neither the national government nor any individual organization will be able to solve the problem of poverty in the Philippines alone (Ababa 2011, 8). It will take a collaborative effort of the government sector, private sector, religious sector and other international parties involved to make significant progress in poverty alleviation. A distrust of the governmental efficiency could be a reason why evangelical Christians in the Philippines have been responding to poverty largely through their local churches, NGOs, and INGOs alone.

Some of the notable evangelical Christian INGOs working in the Philippines are: World Vision, Samaritan's Purse, Compassion International, Food for the Hungry, Christian Aid, Adventist Development and Relief Agency (ADRA), and Global Aid Network (GAIN). Since there are thousands of local evangelical Christian churches and hundreds of NGOs and INGOs that are responding to poverty in the Philippines, they can play a key role in the holistic development of the poor and help alleviate poverty.

In this book, I will focus on select evangelical Christian churches, NGOs, and INGOs from among the whole of the evangelical constituency regarding their response to poverty. I will also share findings from my personal interaction with people in some of the poorest communities in Metro Manila to assess the impact of the evangelical Christian response to poverty.

1

DEFINITION OF TERMS

Three key terms: poverty, development, and evangelical Christian response are frequently used in this book. I have defined them briefly in order to provide consistency in understanding them in the context of this book.

POVERTY

The most common understanding of poverty is a situation where people do not have enough material things to meet their basic needs. According to the so-called poverty line set by the World Bank, people are poor if they make less than two dollars a day. But for evangelical Christians, poverty should not be just an economic and material lack of things. Poverty also extends to the lack of social, psychological, and spiritual needs. As Bryant Myers says, "The way we understand the nature of poverty and what causes poverty is very important, because it tends to determine how we respond to poverty" (Myers 2011, 769). It is important to understand poverty in all its meanings, because people's response to poverty is usually determined by how they understand the term. Therefore, a Christian understanding of poverty must be firmly rooted in the teaching of the Bible in order to provide holistic development of individuals and communities according to God's purpose (Clifford 2010, 9).

Poverty is a situation where a person is not able to afford the very basic necessities for survival. Dirty slums, beggars on the street, children with swollen tummies, barren fields, no electricity, no running water, and no toilet are visible signs of poverty. These are perceptible signs of poverty, but there may be other forms of poverty that are not seen right away. According to UNESCO's definition,

> Poverty is not just economic; it is social, political and cultural. Moreover, it undermines human rights - economic (the right to work and have an adequate income), social (access to health care and education), political (freedom of thought, expression and association) and cultural (the right to maintain one's cultural identity and be involved in a community's cultural life) (Sané 2001, 1).

Therefore, a correct understanding of poverty is very important to help individuals, organizations, and governments understand and implement their poverty alleviation efforts. However, coming up with a universal definition of poverty is almost impossible. According to World Bank,

> Poverty is pronounced deprivation in well-being, and comprises many dimensions. It includes low incomes and the inability to acquire the basic goods and services necessary for survival with dignity. Poverty also encompasses low levels of health and education, poor access to clean water and sanitation, inadequate physical security, lack of voice, and insufficient capacity and opportunity to better one's life (World Bank 2015).

The International Monetary Fund defines poverty as a multidimensional problem that goes beyond economics. Poverty includes social, political, and cultural issues that people face (International Monetary Fund 2001). And, according to the United Nations' definition:

Fundamentally, poverty is a denial of choices and opportunities, a violation of human dignity. It means a lack of basic capacity to participate effectively in society. It means not having enough to feed and clothe a family, not having a school or clinic to go to, not having the land on which to grow one's food or a job to earn one's living and not having access to credit. It means insecurity, powerlessness and exclusion of individuals, households and communities. It means susceptibility to violence and it often implies living in marginal or fragile environments without access to clean water or sanitation (United Nations Economic and Social Council 1998, 1).

Basic food, shelter, medical care, and safety are generally thought necessary based on shared values of human dignity. However, what is a necessity to one person is not always essential to others. Needs may be relative to what is possible and are based on social definition and past experience (Sen 1999, 3). Bryant Myers, a leading evangelical Christian development thinker, talks about five ways in which people have defined poverty. The first definition of poverty is a deficit or lack. People are poor because they are lacking in their basic needs. A second is offered by Robert Chambers who says that poverty is an entanglement of various things. People are poor because they are trapped in this system, which is a cluster of disadvantage. John Friedman presents a third definition, defining poverty as lack of access to social power. People are poor because they are excluded from social access. Jaykumar Christian offers a fourth sense, building onto Chambers' and Friedman's definition by adding the spiritual aspect. He says that poverty is a complex interaction of personal, social, psychological, spiritual, and cultural

systems. The poor are trapped inside the web of these inter-
acting systems. A fifth is by Ravi Jaykaran who defines
poverty as a lack of freedom to grow. He echoes Luke 2:52
and says that people are poor because they are trapped in a
series of restrictions and limitations in physical, mental,
social, and spiritual aspects of life (Myers 2000, 65-72).

DEVELOPMENT

The term development has come a long way since the Second World War as an initiative and as an academic discipline. The idea of development started when certain industrialized countries in the West wanted to help in rebuilding countries in Europe that had been devastated by war. Development was considered as the industrialization of those war-torn countries with the goal to raise income and give poor people access to goods and services (Rapley 2007, 1). In other words, development was about making a better life for everyone. Thus, "The essence of 'development', as most people understand the term, is that it should combat poverty" (Black 2007, 11)

A better life for most people meant meeting basic needs: sufficient food to eat, a safe place to live and proper clothes to wear. It also meant the affordable availability of goods and services to everyone and the dignified treatment of everyone (Peet 2015, 1). Thus, "the idea of development and the possibility of eradication of poverty became the norm in the West" (Myers 2011, 1020). And, according to Wendy R.

Tyndale, "it was often spoken of as a "quasi religious" [sic] mission: as the moral duty of Western industrialized countries to take active steps to help those who are more backward technically (and culturally) to advance along the road of progress" (Tyndale 2006, 156).

In terms of the history of development, Maggie Black writes:

> The idea of development was born not in the developing world, but in the West, as a product of the post-colonial age. Latin American scholars made an important intellectual contribution from the start. The ideas of Mahatma Gandhi of India, Mao Zedong of China, Julius Nyerere of Tanzania and, more recently, of increasing numbers of actors and thinkers in the countries of the South, also played their part. Nonetheless, its evolution in theory and practice has been driven by the industrialized world (Black 2007, 221).

However, even after six decades of development thinking, theorizing, research, policy, and program implementation, there is still increasing inequality and deficiency in the contemporary development process. There is a growing need to revisit the current notions of development, because many development perspectives are only addressing parts of the issue. Moreover, there is a need for a philosophy of development that incorporates economic, psychological, social, and spiritual well-being of the poor. According to Gilbert Rist, "Development consists of a set of practices, sometimes appearing to conflict with one another, which require – for the reproduction of society – the general transformation and destruction of the natural environment and of social relations. Its aim is to increase the production of commodities (goods and services) geared, by way of exchange, to effective demand" (Rist 2008, 13).

The early definitions of development and theories of development focused mainly on economics. And those early definitions and theories are the ones adopted by most Asian countries. Development, however, is a comprehensive process of economic, psychological, social, cultural, political, and spiritual progress that continually improves the well-being of the community or nation as a whole and all of its individuals. In terms of evangelical Christian participation in development, it began after the 1960s when the United Nations declared the 1960s as the "decade of development." Until then, evangelicals were primarily involved in relief work in their expression of social concern for the poor (relief work refers to providing immediate needs in desperate situations).

By the mid 1970s, development became a major activity of the evangelical missionary agenda with the traces of modernization and dependency theory. Many evangelical relief agencies then became relief and development agencies in order to incorporate development in their work (Tizon 2008, 35-36). Ruth Callanta defines development in her chapter, "A Transformational Strategy: Filling the Hungry with Good Things" in the book *The Church and Poverty in Asia,* in this way:

> Development, for me, then goes beyond merely giving more to the poor, beyond adding to who they are and what they have. Rather, I understand development to mean helping the poor change into

better, fulfilled, and more productive individuals –
like caterpillars transforming into butterflies. But
this transformation must be centered on Jesus Christ
(Callanta 2008, 149).

EVANGELICAL CHRISTIAN RESPONSE

The term "evangelical" refers to someone who believes in the Gospel. In addition to that, an evangelical is someone who has a "burning passion for the communication of the Gospel" (Costas 1986, 312). Timothy George argues that evangelicals are:

> A worldwide family of Bible-believing Christians committed to sharing with everyone everywhere the transforming good news of new life in Jesus Christ, an utterly free gift that comes through faith alone in the crucified and risen Savior. ...Evangelicals are gospel people and Bible people. We do not claim to be the only true Christians, but we recognize in one another a living, personal trust in Jesus the Lord, and this is the basis of our fellowship across to so many ethnic, cultural, national, and denominational divides (George 1999, 62).

Thus the phrase "evangelical Christian" in this book refers to all Christians who believe that salvation is by grace through faith in Jesus Christ, and are actively involved in proclamation and demonstration of the Gospel. In the context of the Philippines, evangelical Christians refer to Christians affiliated with Philippine Council of Evangelical Churches (PCEC), Christians from mainline churches, Christians from Pentecostal and charismatic churches, and Christians from other independent churches.

Evangelical Christians have typically been visible in responding to poverty in many ways, though they hold various views on the problem of poverty and its causes. Some believe that responding to poverty is not something every Christian should do; instead it has to be given to the development professionals. Others believe that every Christian should play a part in responding to poverty. Thus, it is worth reflecting on the range of evangelical Christian understanding of poverty before examining their response to it (Clifford 2010, 6). Tim Chester writes in his book, *Good News to the Poor: Social Involvement and the Gospel*, that evangelical Christians should accept the fact that they cannot eradicate poverty. However, it should not be an excuse because they still have an obligation to care of the poor. Proclaiming the Gospel is central to evangelical Christian response to poverty because the real need of the poor is to be reconciled with God, but the message they proclaim is best understood in the context of loving actions (Chester 2013, 192).

In terms of evangelical Christian response to poverty, one of the well-known, yet often-misunderstood phrase that Jesus said is: "The poor you will always have with you." Some have even gone to the extreme of taking it as an excuse to completely ignore the poor. Thus, it is crucial to look at this phrase in its original context in Deuteronomy 15:11 and in the Gospels (Matthew 26:11, Mark 14:7, and John

12:8). Jesus referred to Deuteronomy 15:11: "There will always be poor people in the land. Therefore I command you to be openhanded toward your fellow Israelites who are poor and needy in your land" (NIV) when he said, "The poor you will always have with you, but you will not always have me" (NIV). So, in Deuteronomy 15:11 when God said, "There will always be poor people in the land," He was actually referring to his command to the Israelites to take care of their fellow brothers and sisters in need. In Deuteronomy 15:4-5 God said, "However, there need be no poor people among you, for in the land the Lord your God is giving you to possess as your inheritance, he will richly bless you, if only you fully obey the Lord your God and are careful to follow all these commands I am giving you today" (NIV). And in the context of the Gospels, Jesus commended the devotion of the woman when she anointed him with a very expensive perfume. Her action symbolized that Jesus is Messiah and it also prepared him for his burial. So, Jesus told the disciples that he would not be around anymore, but the poor people will be around for them to take care of (Keller Jr. 2012, 407-408).

"Although the Bible is not a textbook on poverty alleviation, it does give us valuable insights into the nature of human beings, of history, of culture, and of God to point us in the right direction" (Corbett and Fikkert 2013, 53). God is concerned about the poor; thus, his commands for his people to respond to the needs of the poor are found throughout the Bible. "The reality of poverty in our world places specific obligations upon all Christians for showing mercy in our various capacities as neighbors, church members, citizens, and those who are wealthy" (Bolt 2013, 2584).

Jesus was deeply concerned about the poor too. In Luke

4:18-19 he says, "The Spirit of the Lord is on me, because he
has anointed me to proclaim good news to the poor. He has
sent me to proclaim freedom for the prisoners and recovery
of sight for the blind, to set the oppressed free, to proclaim
the year of the Lord's favor" (NIV). He is compassionate to
the poor. When the large crowds gathered to listen to him
became hungry and his disciples suggested that he send
them away to buy food, Jesus had compassion for those
hungry people. In Mark 8:2 Jesus said to his disciples, "I
have compassion for these people; they have already been
with me three days and have nothing to eat" (NIV). Then he
performed miracles to feed them (Nowers, Burt and Randy
Steger 2013, 1).

Thus, Jesus reminds Christians to respond to the poor
when he says in Matthew 25:40, "Whatever you did for one
of the least of these brothers and sisters of mine, you did for
me." He associated with "tax collectors, and sinners",
welcomed the company of women and children, and others
held in low esteem in the culture of His time. These people
were the object of many of his healing miracles, and they
took their place among his followers. The actions of Jesus
are in themselves good news for the poor, and are great
examples for an evangelical Christian response to poverty.
Since evangelical Christians believe that God cares for the
poor, they should care for the poor too. Ronald J Sider
writes in his book, *Rich Christians in an Age of Hunger: Moving
from Affluence to Generosity*, "Since God cares so much for the
poor, it is hardly surprising that God wants his people to do
the same" (Sider 2015, 61).

A typical evangelical Christian understanding of poverty
is that people are poor because they are separated from
God. People of this persuasion understand the causes and
effects of poverty in relational terms. According to Bryant

Myers, a leading evangelical Christian development thinker and practitioner, "poverty is the absence of shalom in all its meanings" (Myers 2000, 86-87). He refers to the absence of shalom as the condition where people's relationship with God, with self, with others, and with rest of God's creation is not right. Lisa Sharon Harper describes that relationship in this way:

> Humanity's broken relationship with God is the ultimate cause of all other brokenness. In another sense, there is no way humanity could violate relationship with any other created being and not violate its relationship with God. Creating is bound together by relationship with our Creator since it is Creator God's love that binds us together. To break one tie is to break them all (Harper 2016, 61).

Many evangelical Christians respond to the problem of poverty with the intention to reconcile people to God. They also believe that the church should not stand and watch poverty around the world without seeking to do anything about it, instead, the church should work for justice, fairness, and hope for the poor who are hopeless and helpless. Thus, they respond to the poor with care and compassion which Jesus himself demonstrated (Christian Aid 2011, 1).

Evangelical Christians are recognizing the emotional, soul, and heart dimensions of poverty that relates to the love and compassion to the poor. The "Manila Manifesto" of "Lausanne Movement" calls evangelicals to "demonstrate God's love visibly by caring for those who are deprived of justice, dignity, food and shelter." Likewise, the Micah Network has issued the call for evangelical Christians to using Micah 6:8: "commit ourselves, as followers of Jesus, to work together for the holistic transformation of our communities, to act justly, to love mercy and to walk humbly with our God" (Christian 2011, 1679). Evangelical Christian response to poverty is a result of their understanding that Jesus identifies with the poor. He was born in an insignificant province of the Roman Empire. His parents could not afford to bring a lamb for purification, which is why they brought two pigeons to the temple. Jesus worked as a carpenter to sustain himself and to support his family. He neither had his own house nor had a regular income during his public ministry. Thus, he warned his followers in Matthew 8:20 (NIV), "Foxes have dens and birds have nests, but the Son of Man has no place to lay his head" (Sider 2015, 53).

Evangelical Christians have been visible in responding to poverty in the Philippines since 1899 through the establishment of YMCA as it opened the door for Protestant missions and missionaries. Presbyterians pioneered in medical work, higher education, and Protestant mission cooperation. They also established the first Protestant school in the Philippines, Silliman Institute (now Silliman University) (Moffett, Samuel H. 2005, 559-560). However, the persistence of poverty shows that there is so much more to be done. So, this book provides insights from various perspectives in order to clarify and solidify evangelical Christian response to poverty.

2

CAUSES OF POVERTY

U nderstanding the underlying causes of poverty is the most important thing to do in responding to poverty. It is impossible to even think of solving the problem of poverty without going to its roots. There are numerous causes of poverty around the world as they vary from one country to other. The causes of poverty that I have included in this book are the main causes of poverty in the Philippines.

POPULATION GROWTH

Population growth is believed to be one of the main causes of persistent poverty in the Philippines. The chart below shows the population of the Philippines from 1990 to 2015. The figures are shown in millions from the particular years when a census was taken.

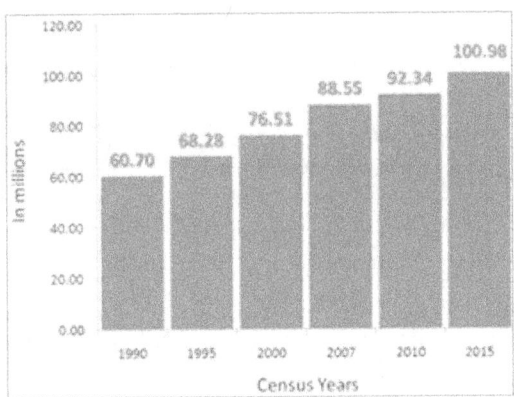

It is evident that the population of the Philippines has been growing rapidly over the years. If this growth continues until 2020, the population will have almost doubled over the span of 30 years. The population has been growing, but the resources and government capability is not growing in the same ratio. Population growth would not be a problem if the resources and systems were in place to sustain it. But, in the context of the Philippines, lack of resources and unjust political system make it difficult for the poor to get out of their situation. Since the population growth rate is usually high in poor communities, poor people are having a hard time getting out of poverty cycle. Thus, this fast-paced population growth is arguably one of the reasons behind the persistence of poverty in the Philippines over the years.

The Filipino economy is growing, but that growth is not being felt by those on the lowest incomes. Some of this can be attributed to the country's rapid population growth. The country simply does not have enough money to take enough people out of poverty (ASEAN Today 2018). The table below show the percentage of the total population of the Philippines below the poverty line from 1997 to 2015.

Country	1997	2001	2003	2006	2009	2015
Philippines	41	40	30	32.9	26.5	21.6

(Source: CIA World Factbook)

The average percentage of the total population below the poverty line during that period of time was 32%. Poverty seems to have slightly declined as result of recent growth. However, the slow rate of poverty reduction has affected the country's economic development" (ADB 2009,1136).

RECURRING NATURAL DISASTERS

One of the factors to consider regarding the problem of poverty in the Philippines is the reality of recurring natural disasters. Some of the examples are: the 7.7 magnitude earthquake that hit Baguio city in 1990, the eruption of Mount Pinatubo in 1991, mudslides in Southern Leyte in 2003, flooding and mudslides in Quezon province in 2004, mudslides in southern Leyte in 2005, and typhoon "Reming" that hit Bicol in 2006 (Wanak 2008, 197). Typhoon "Ondoy" in 2009 and super typhoon "Juan" in 2010 hit Luzon leaving thousands dead and billions of Philippine pesos in loss. According to the Citizens' Disaster Response Center (CDRC), "the Philippines topped the list of countries most frequently hit by natural disasters in 2011."

Natural disasters are beyond human control, but there are preventive measures that can be taken by the frequent disaster victims and by the government. Majority of the slum dwellers in Metro Manila came from various provinces as a result being affected by frequent natural disasters. Since most of those who get affected by natural disasters are the poor people, it forces them into the poverty cycle.

LACK OF EDUCATION

Lack of education is one of the key factors that keep the poverty persistent in the Philippines. Though Filipinos have high literacy rates, poverty levels in the Philippines remain disproportionately high" (ASEAN Today 2018). It shows that being literate does not guarantee a way out of poverty. People need education in order to get out of poverty.

Poverty and education are inextricably linked, because people living in poverty may stop going to school so they can work, which leaves them without literacy and numeracy skills they need to further their careers. Their children, in turn, are in a similar situation years later, with little income and few options but to leave school and work (ChildFund 2018).

Currently, 6.2 million primary-school aged children are not in school. Many of them are forced out of school so they could work and support their family. There are several factors that affect their education, such as: lack of school supplies, lack of teachers, lack of food, and natural disasters. All of these hindering factors are either a cause or a result of poverty (Save Children Philippines 2018).

In addition to the lack of education, lack of financial literacy is another key factor that contributes to the persistence of poverty. "Only 25 percent of Filipino adults are financially literate, a Standard & Poor's (S&P) Ratings Services survey found, highlighting the challenges facing the goal of boosting access to financial services" (The Manila Times 2015).

CORRUPTION

Aside from population growth, recurring natural disasters, and lack of education, corruption contributes to the persistent poverty in the Philippines. In fact, "Corruption has been described as 'chronic' in the Philippines" (ADB 2009, 1164). The chart below shows the ranking of the Philippines based on the Transparency International's Corruption Perceptions Index from 2012 to 2017.

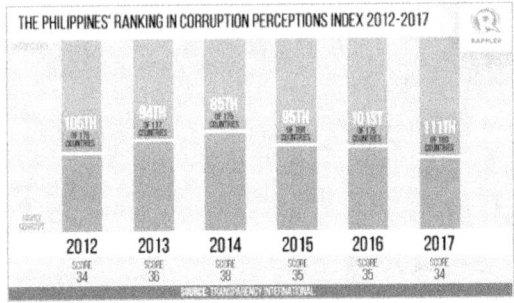

THE PHILIPPINES' RANKING IN CORRUPTION PERCEPTIONS INDEX 2012-2017

Transparency International scores 170 plus countries each year to show the level of corruption in their public sector. It uses the scale of 0 to 100, where 0 is highly corrupt and 100 is very clean. It is evident that corruption in the Philippines is high as the average score in the past five years is 35. According to the 2013 National Household Survey on Experience with Corruption in the Philippines conducted by the office of Ombudsman, "poverty exists partly because of corruption." Ruben C. De Lara, president and CEO of Serving Humanity through Empowerment and Development (SHED) Inc., writes in the Manila Times, "Corruption and poverty are two sides of the same coin. Ending one can help end the other."

3

SOCIOECONOMIC DEVELOPMENT THEORIES

S ocioeconomic development is the process of social and economic development, which can be measured with social and economic indicators like; gross domestic product (GDP), life expectancy, literacy and levels of employment. Social and economic aspects are insepa-rable in the understanding of socioeconomic development. They are like two sides of a coin and together they define the identity and value of that coin. In many development discourses, the coin of socioeconomic development is defined with the understanding of only one side, which is the economic development. But to recognize the real worth of the coin of socioeconomic development, both social and economic sides of development must be considered. Gener-ally, the low living standard of the masses in developing countries is seen as the key issue of development. However, socioeconomic development of developing countries is a dynamic interplay between economic and social factors (Szirmai 2015, 1).

Social development is a process that results in the trans-formation of social institutions. It also improves the capacity of a society to fulfill its aspirations. Economic development on the other hand, is a process by which a nation progresses on the economic, political, and social well-being of its people. In addition to social and economic aspects, it also includes political and environmental well-being of the people. Socioeconomic development is about the overall quality of life that people enjoy in a country.

Thus, the study of socioeconomic development is a truly interdisciplinary venture and comprehensive process. It crosses the established boundaries of academic social science to analyze the causes and consequences of social change. Socioeconomic development forms individual belief systems, cultural patterns, economic institutions, methods of manufacturing and distributing goods and services, socio-political arrangements, and international economy (Jaffee 1998, 59).

According to James Midgley, the connection of social interventions with economic activities is not new. In the 1930s, British colonial authorities began to change their policies and promoted economic development in Western Africa. And in the 1940s, the economic development was reinforced by efforts in education and social services. It was only in 1954 that the British adopted the term "social development" to describe their economic, educational, and social services. In the beginning of the 1960s, The United Nations (UN) started using social development for their economic and social welfare services. In the 1960s, some of the prominent economists endorsed the idea of unified socioeconomic development planning and recommended central planning agencies, which gave birth to the concept of socioeconomic development.

But in the 1980s, the idea of close connection between social and economic development was slowly fading in the

U.S. and Western Europe. Some of the gains made in the previous decades on integrating social and economic development efforts were lost. As a result, development plans in the Global South were implemented, focusing only on economic growth with a strong belief that social development would inevitably follow economic development (Fritz, 3).

This influenced both the Global South academicians and foreign advisers to newly independent countries, whose confidence in the government was further reinforced by the rise of structuralist economics. Being aware of the flaws in the world economy and being confident that the government could overcome them, development theorists proposed models that gave those newly independent nations a leading role in their economy. Many third-world governments adopted those models of state-led economy for a quick journey into the industrial age (Rapley 2007, 2-3).

While the idea of development suggests a process of becoming a more developed nation, development theories explain how this process takes place. The history of theorizing about development goes back to the writings of classical economists such as Adam Smith, Marx, Engels, and Friedrich. But the recent development of development theories took place in the middle of the twentieth century.

Today there are numerous theories of socioeconomic development. How one would wish development scholars would just agree on the best theory and tell the world. But, in reality, it is not as simple as that, because socioeconomic development theories reflect the diversity of people's perspective of development. Their political, philosophical, economic, and geographic perspectives have a significant influence in creating those theories.

Throughout the 20th century and moving into the 21st

century, western governments have tried their best to help develop the poor countries. And, they have used various development theories in the process. As a result of those development efforts, many countries experienced growth in their national income, and many poor people around the world were lifted out of poverty. However, western governments continue to have diverse views in terms of developing the poor countries in the world (Harriss 2014, 7).

Following are the six key theories of socioeconomic development that have guided development discourse since the 1960s to the present day:

MODERNIZATION THEORY

The modern era of development began with an idea that the world, particularly developing countries, could be developed within a few generations. "The idea of modernization is primarily an American idea, developed by American social scientists in the period after the Second World War and reaching the height of its popularity in the middle years of the 1960s" (Tipps 1976, 71).

This notion emphasized the modernization of backward economics in order to eliminate poverty. It later became known as modernization theory, which identifies the reasons behind development in the First World countries and provides suggestions in terms of what, why and where the Third World countries are lacking. This concept also suggests that a fundamental mechanism drives the movement of societies through various stages (Rapely 2007, 16).

There were three main events that helped in laying the foundation of modernization theory after World War II. The first event was the rise of the United States as a superpower. It happened at the time when Great Britain, France, and Germany were weakened by their involvement and investment in the war. The United States initiated rebuilding war-torn Western Europe by implementing the Marshall Plan. The second was the spread of the communist movement around the world. The Soviet Union expanded its communist influence to China and Korea in addition to Eastern Europe.

The third event was the collapse of European colonies in Asia, Africa, and Latin America. It gave birth to many new nation-states around the world. Those emerging nation-states were in search of a model of development to promote their economy and to enhance their political independence. They considered rich western European nations as their model and started modernizing themselves to be like the west (Reyes 2001, 2). Thus, "Modernization theory originated from the so-called behavioral revolution, a shift in U.S. social scientific thought that began in the late 1940s and continued through the 1960s" (Rapely 2007 16).

Nature and Scope of Modernization Theory

Modernization theory is based on Walt Rostow's five stages of the economic development model. Rostow was an economist and special assistant to U.S. President Johnson, whose ideas on free trade and modernization were very influential in the 1960s.

> According to his exposition, Rostow has found a possible solution for the promotion of Third World modernization. If the problem facing Third World countries resides in their lack of productive investments, then the solution lies the provision of aid to these countries in the form of capital, technology, and expertise. The "Marshall Plan" and the "Alliance for Progress in Latin America" are

examples of programs which were influenced by Rostow's political theories (Royal Geographical Society with IBG 2013).

He argues that science and technology should be maximized to advance industry and stimulate economic growth. Development will then be achieved when a country has high industrial productivities and exports goods to the rest of the world. Modernization provides third-world governments with a clear course for development to follow that is based on the rich first world governments. Modernization produces economic growth to increase living standards of the poor (Royal Geographical Society with IBG 2013).

According to Gilbert Rist, "modernization is only a form of Westernization" (Rist 2008, 102). Modernization by nature is a homogenizing process that produces inclinations toward resemblance among societies. For developing countries, modernization is all about Europeanization or Americanization because they look up to Europe and America as their model for economic prosperity and democratic stability. As a result, modernization becomes an unending process for the poor countries. Once poor countries come into contact with the Western countries, they will not be able to resist the temptation toward modernization (Reyes 2016).

Modernization theory is based on optimistic economic growth models. The Western countries that are economically rich serve as a model for this theory. And the poor countries are believed to be in their initial state of economic growth. Modernization theory proponents focus on choosing the right techniques and technologies designed by Western countries to achieve industrialization in the poor countries. They emphasizes the importance of lending capital to entrepreneurs and providing education in capitalist values. Bryant Myers describes the nature of his theory in this way:

> In the 1960s Walt Rostow's "non-Communist manifesto" and his five stages of economic growth became the blueprint for Western development strategies of the time (1960). The goal of development was understood as modernization (westernization) and the measure of development was the size of a nation's economy. Making economics grow by following Rostow's five stages of economic growth was the means of development (Myers 2011, 1022).

As a result of entrepreneurship, proponents of the theory hold that national income will grow which will then lead to maximum economic growth. Modernization theorists see development as a process that was led by the historical example of the rise of Western countries.

In this view, the rest of the countries in the world are just trying to catch up with the Western countries. Modernization focuses on the improvement of the political and economic capacities of non-western countries. And the influence of industrialization of the western countries will encourage those poor countries to focus on their own economic growth. As a result of modernization, there will be an increase in urbanization, labor specialization, educational expansion, change of value-systems and other social changes. In this sense, modernization is a shift from the Marxist focus on economic issues to a focus on cultural and ideological dimensions (Foote 2014, 8-9).

Limitations of Modernization Theory
Modernization theory was popular in the early and mid-

1960s but came under heavy attack at the end of the 1960s. There were several criticisms of the modernization theory. The first was this:

> Rostow failed to consider that an economy could reach the fifth stage without going through all the stages or a particular sequence. For instance, it has been pointed out that countries like Canada and Australia entered the stage of mass consumption even before reaching the stage of maturity (Reyes 2016).

Secondly, modernization theory only shows one particular model of development. The example is the development pattern of the United States. But it is evident that there have been development advances in other nations, such as Taiwan, Singapore, Hong Kong and South Korea. In addition, their existing development levels have been achieved by strong authoritarian regimes. Thirdly, modernization theory rejects traditional values and recommends replacement with modern values of the west. In contrast, China and Japan, despite their advances in economic development, continue to operate with traditional values (Reyes 2016). And the fourth criticism of modernization theory is that the term modernization itself is vague. It has been used simply as a synonym for industrialization. It deserves no functionality as a theoretical framework, which makes modernization theory questionable. Because of the vague and ambiguous use of the term, modernization theory has lost its originality (Rahaman 2014).

DEPENDENCY THEORY

Dependency theory is about the socioeconomic development of a country based on the political, economic, and
cultural influences of other countries. Dependency theory
came as a response to the modernization theory in the 1970s.
Proponents of the modernization theory have argued that,
in order for the non-western poor countries to develop, they
should change their traditional ways and follow western
values. It also claims that countries that are still focusing on
the agricultural sector would be identified as a backward
country. So, the dependency theory was born to respond to
the modernization theory promoted by the rich Western
countries (Dang 2015, 18).

Andre Gunder Frank, one of the key proponents of
dependency theory, argues that some western countries
have become winners of global trade while the majority of
the non-western countries have been losers. Those winning
western countries have become wealthy by exploiting and
inhibiting development of the non-western countries
through unfair trade. He sees the world being divided into
two regions, calling one region 'core' and the other region

'periphery.' The core region is made up of developed countries: North American and Western European countries. And the periphery region is made up of underdeveloped countries mostly in the third world.

The core and the periphery have different functions in the global economic system. Resources flow into the core from the periphery for industrial production. Then the high-value goods flow back to the periphery for consumption. Frank argues that this imbalanced structure of the world economic system makes the core richer and the periphery poorer. As a result of this economic imbalance, poor non-western countries are dependent on the rich western countries for their development (Royal Geographical Society with IBG 2013).

Dependency theory's root goes back to the 1950s when Paul Baran first brought it to light through his writing, *The Political Economy of Growth*. Yet, only a decade later dependency theory began to flourish. Andre Gunder Frank later sharpened Baran's analysis, stressing that development and underdevelopment were two sides of the same coin (Rapely 2007, 18). The foundations of dependency theory were strengthened by the research done by the Economic Commission for Latin America and the Caribbean (ECLAC). Raul Prebisch was one of the most representative authors who provided the basis for the proposal for dependency theory. There were several other key proponents such as Theotonio Dos Santos, Enrique Cardozo, Edelberto Torres-Rivas, and Samir Amin (Reyes 2016). Theotonio Dos Santos emphasizes the historical dimension of dependency relationships. He says,

> Dependency is a historical condition which shapes a certain structure of the world economy such that it

favors some countries to the detriment of others and limits the development possibilities of the subordinate economics...a situation in which the economy of a certain group of countries is conditioned by the development and expansion of another economy, to which their own is subjected (Ferraro 2008, 58-64).

The history of dependency theory shows that the developed Western countries are always in the center and the developing Third World countries are in the periphery. And it argues that the center has exploited the periphery through colonialism, imperialism, and dependent capitalism (Lal 2002, 91).

From the very beginning of dependency thinking, most dependency theorists have agreed on certain common features. First, they describe the world economic system as comprised of two groups of countries that are contrasted as dominant vs. dependent, center vs. periphery, and metropolitan vs. satellite. The dominant countries are usually the industrialized countries in Western Europe, while the dependent countries are usually the countries in Latin America, Asia, and Africa. These dependent countries are poor and rely heavily on their export of a particular product for income. Secondly, its proponents express the importance of external forces that are necessary for the economic growth of the dependent countries. These external forces could be multinational corporations, access to international markets, foreign assistance, communications, and new technologies. The industrialized countries in the core can easily manipulate their economic interests in those poor countries in the periphery. And thirdly, advocates of dependency theory describe the relationship between the dominant and the dependent countries, which is so intense and dynamic that it leads to unequal patterns. Besides, dependency is a deeply seated historical process that is rooted in the internationalization of the concept of capitalism. Today, the poor periphery countries are still trapped by large debts that prevent them from developing. Therefore, dependency was and is still an ongoing process in the area of socioeconomic development (Ferraro 2008, 58-64).

Nature and Scope of Dependency Theory

Dependency theorists typically study the colonial impact on the socio-economic and political structures in underdeveloped countries that are in periphery. They go on to examine the characteristics of their new socio-economic structure after the colonial period. And finally they trace its development progress in the context of the world capitalist economic system. Proponents claim that underdevelopment of the underdeveloped countries is intimately and inseparably related to their external dependence on the capitalist developed countries (Dinesh 2015). Adam Szirmai suggests that the term "dependence" indicates that development in poor countries in the periphery is dependent on the development in rich countries in the core. And, that dependence is not limited to the economic sphere; it extends to cultural, psychological, and political dependence (Szirmai 2015, 97).

Thus, it is helpful to understand some of those underlying factors of dependency in order to comprehend the nature and scope of the theory. Dependency theory arose as a reaction to modernization theory. Its advocates argue that Western countries do not guide the underdeveloped countries out of backwardness as the modernization theory claims. They further claim that, in fact, modernization theory is hindering the development of the underdeveloped countries (Rapley 2007, 21). Supporters argue that dominance of the developed countries over developing countries creates underdevelopment. Underdevelopment is a condition in which resources of the developing countries are being actively used but the developed countries enjoy the benefit of those resources, keeping the developing countries poor. It also leads the developing countries to dependence on the developed countries for market and capital.

Dependency theorists believe that free trade has become a tool for the developed countries to manipulate poor countries. And multinational corporations are also key players in making the developing countries become more dependent on the developed countries. But the benefit of that dependency to the developing countries is very minimal compared to the benefits that developed countries get. As a result, developing countries cannot even expect socioeconomic development from that dependence. Therefore, proponents of the dependency theory suggest that countries in the periphery should end their dependence on the core countries by breaking up their relationships (Dang 2015, 18).

Advocates of dependency theory argue that the developing countries are not behind or catching up to the developed countries. And they are not poor because they did not follow the methods and values of the developed countries. They are poor because they were forcefully integrated into the western economic system only as producers of raw materials and as sources of cheap labor. They did not have the freedom to market their resources in any way that competed with developed countries. Proponents advocate that the relationship between developing and developed countries should be a voluntary relationship for mutual benefit, not a forceful relationship for one party's benefit

(Ferraro 2008, 58-64). And to have such mutual partnership for mutual benefit, dependency theorists suggest that the control of the global system by the developed countries should be weakened through trade barriers. There should also be control on big multi–national corporations so that the raw materials and cheap labor of developing countries are not exploited. On the other hand, developing countries should form regional trading areas to buy and sell their raw materials and finished products. Dependency theory exponents believe that self–reliance and local community-driven development is the key to socioeconomic development of developing countries (Dang 2015, 18).

Limitations of Dependency Theory

One of the major limitations of the dependency theory is that it does not clearly define and explain dependence and underdevelopment. It also does not suggest an acceptable standard to differentiate the dependent countries from the non-dependent countries. According to S.K. Sahu, "The authors of the dependency theory have concerned themselves with attacking the desirability of the capitalist-system in the periphery rather than the dependent status." Proponents emphasize the flaws of capitalism instead of emphasizing the ways and means for ending dependency. Another limitation is that its advocates analyze the nature of underdevelopment of all the Third-World countries in the same way. They fail to realize that underdevelopment in Asia is very different from the underdevelopment of Africa and Latin America. And in many cases, underdeveloped countries themselves are responsible for their dependency on capitalist countries (Dinesh 2015).

Another criticism of dependency theory is that it does not provide comprehensive practical evidence to support its conclusions. It has the tendency to remain as a theoretical position that uses highly abstract levels of analysis. Another limitation is that its theorists consider relationship with multinational corporations as unfavorable to the developing countries. In reality, these relationships can be used as a means of acquiring new technology. They tend to forget that even the United States was once a colony of European countries. And, the US was able to come out of that underdevelopment to become one of the most developed countries (Reyes 2016). One of the major limitations of the dependency theory is that it fails to show the changes in the socio-economic and political situations of the developing countries.

NEOLIBERALISM THEORY

Neoliberalism, in many ways, is a revitalization of liberalism. Liberalism was absent from political discussions and policy-making for a long period of time, and it emerged in a reincarnated form. It has gone through a process of initial growth, intermediate decline, and finally came a renewal. Thus, neoliberalism is usually thought of as the return and spread of one specific aspect of liberalism (Thorsen 2007, 15). Neoliberalism took significant shape in the 1970s as a distinctive political–economic philosophy. Proponents were committed to the expansion of market-like forms of governance, rule, and control in all spheres of social life. A significant moment in the history of neoliberalism occurred with the 1973 coup in Chile, and the election of Margaret Thatcher in the United Kingdom and Ronald Reagan in the United States. In their own ways, these governments took significant steps to establish an order in which the barriers to finance-oriented accumulation were either minimized or removed. As a result, early stages of the neoliberalism were characterized by acts of institutional reaction and political repression (Leitner 2007, 15-16).

The word "neoliberalism" has gone through a significant change from its roots in Germany to its modern usage. It was coined by the economists at the German Freiberg School as an alternative to classical liberalism. Modern day scholars often use neoliberalism negatively as they associate it with free market fundamentalism. However, the economic philosophers of the German Freiberg School used it in a positive sense as they believed in the free market. They further explained the key role of the nation in order for the free market to function well (Boas and Gans-Morse 2009, 145-46).

The first systematic formulation of the concept of neoliberalism goes back to the Mont Pelerin Society founded in 1947 by Friedrich August von Hayek. He mobilized several other scholars to reinforce the principles and practices of free society that is based on market-oriented economic systems. He wanted to revive classical liberalism in their attempt to challenge the dominance of Keynesian ideas. Hayek believed that accurate price mechanism allows people to achieve diverse ends without state interference. He believed that economic freedom was a political and moral force that played a key role in shaping all other aspects of a free society. As a result, there was the rise of the first-wave of neoliberalism in the English-speaking world which is associated with U.S. president Ronald Regan and British Prime Minister Margaret Thatcher.They implemented neoliberal ideology into their public policies and programs.

American economist Milton Friedman, who was greatly influenced by Hayek's neoliberal principles, played a significant role in making neoliberalism the ruling economic view in the 1990s. His theory of monetarism suggested that "only the self-regulating free market allowed for the right number of goods at correct prices produced by workers paid at wage levels determined by the free market" (Steger 2010, 17). Friedman suggested that central banks like the US Federal Reserve should implement anti-inflationary policies to keep the supply and demand of money balanced. There was a second-wave of neoliberalism, which is associated with U.S. president Bill Clinton and British Prime Minister Tony Blair. They implemented a revolutionary blend of market-oriented thinking and moderate social policies. Thus, neoliberalism, formulated by prominent neoliberal economists, quickly spread all over the world (Steger 2010, 14-19).

Nature and Scope of Neoliberalism Theory

Neoliberalism is considered as a theory of political economic practices. Its advocates propose that promoting individual entrepreneurial potentials best advances human well-being. And to promote such political economic practices and individual potentials, the state should provide private property rights, free markets, and free trade. It should also set up military, defense, police, and legal structures and functions required in securing private property rights so as to allow the markets to properly function (Harvey 2005, 2). Neoliberalism theorists claim that free market and free global trade can stimulate economic growth and large corporations can benefit more without governmental intervention.

Proponents also argue that with no trade taxes, goods can be bought worldwide at low costs and multinational corporations can freely invest overseas with no trade barriers in order to promote competitive businesses. Proponents strongly advocate that global development is possible through global trade, not aid (Royal Geographical Society with IBG 2013). Neoliberalism proponents also argue that free markets and free trade will also promote creative potential and the entrepreneurial spirit of the entrepreneurs. It will lead to individual freedom and well-being, and at the same time, well-organized distribution of resources.

Defenders of neoliberalism argue that the state should protect individual, commercial, liberty, as well as strong private property rights. The theory also provides a perspective on moral virtue of the individuals, as they are responsible for the results of their choices. It says that the virtuous person "is able to access the relevant markets and function as a competent actor in these markets. He or she is willing to accept the risks associated with participating in free markets and to adapt to rapid changes..." (Thorsen 2007, 15).

Neoliberalism is often viewed as synonymous with the Washington Consensus which refers to the lowest common denominator of policy advice given mostly to Latin American countries by IMF, World Bank and other international financial institutions based in Washington. In the 1990s, the Washington Consensus became the global framework for economic development that led many countries to development. It was later exported to the rest of the developing world with the requirement to adhere to its ten-point program (Steger 2010, 21).

Neoliberalism advocates argue that it is usually the government that prevents development. They talk about the regimes in Eastern Europe to show how governments can impede development. Eastern European governments prohibited their people from bringing the consumer culture that began in Western Europe in the 1960s. Those governments had too much power to control the market, which resulted in the stagnation of development.

Advocates of this theory also argue that even in capitalist countries where there are too many rules, regulations and taxes, it is harder to do business and economic development is more difficult. Neoliberalism theorists insist that developing countries should remove barriers to free market capitalism and allow capitalism to help in the process of development (Siddiqui 2012, 15). Thus, the purpose of neoliberalism was to promote a mechanism for efficient global trade and investment, which would open the door for all nations to prosper and develop.

Limitations of Neoliberalism Theory

One of the limitations of neoliberalism is the fact that its proponents are tremendously skeptical of democracy. They look at governments with a majority rule as a possible threat to individual rights and constitutional liberties. For them, democracy is a luxury that is only possible in developed countries that are rich. Neoliberalists tend to favor governance by experts and elites. They would prefer executive orders and judicial decisions rather than democratic and parliamentary decision-making process.

Another limitation of neoliberalism is the problem in interpreting monopoly power. "Competition often results in monopoly or oligopoly, as stronger firms drive out weaker. Most neoliberal theorists consider this unproblematic (it should, they say, maximize efficiency) provided there are no substantial barriers to the entry of competitors (a condition often hard to realize and which the state may therefore have to nurture) (Harvey 2005, 67). Their suggestion of the so-called "natural monopolies" does no work in the developing countries.

Another major area of limitation of neoliberalism pertains to market failure. This happens when individuals

and firms do no pay the full costs by shedding their obligations outside the market. Proponents of neoliberalism
presume that there will be perfect information and a level
playing field for competition, which is an idealist assumption. One of the limitations of neoliberalism is that the
freedom of the poor people is regulated in favor of the freedoms of the few rich people in the country (Harvey 2005,
66-67).

The theorists of neoliberalism promote a very limited
role for the state than even most conservative programs
envisioned prior to the late 1970s. Neoliberalism's geography
is different from previous pro-market initiatives and it is
seen as a global project that has been accepted by elites and
politicians around the world. "Those countries that have
adopted free market polices have developed more slowly
than those that protected their economies. Dependency
theorists argue that neoliberalism is merely a way to open
up countries so they are more easily exploited by Transnational Corporations" (Leitner, Peck and Sheppard 2007, 91).
Thus, one of the limitations of neoliberalism is that the
multinational corporations usually do not invest in the
poorest countries of the world; rather, they invest in moder-
ately underdeveloped countries (Leitner, Peck and Sheppard 2007, 91).

Another limitation of neoliberalism is its focus on the
market to find a way out of poverty for the developing countries. National policies of liberalization, stabilization and
privatization are some of the fundamental elements for
economic development. Though foreign trade and
international investments are flowing into the developing
countries, they have not brought about the expected results
for the poorest ones. Therefore, many conclude that

because of diverse institutional, governmental, cultural, and historical context of the poorest countries, a free market fails to stimulate economic development within them (Dang 2015, 19).

SUSTAINABLE DEVELOPMENT THEORY

Sustainable development has been a popular phrase in the development discourse in the recent years. Sustainable development theory is the combination of environmental and socioeconomic concerns. It focuses on solving environmental and socioeconomic challenge that the world is facing today by being considerate to the needs of the future generations (Hopwood 2005, 38). The first important use of the term sustainable development was in 1980 in the World Conservation Strategy to bring together environmental and socio-economic issues. In 1987, the influential Brundtland Report written for the United Nations presented the definition and framework for sustainable development: "Sustainable development is defined as development that meets the needs of the present without compromising the ability of future generations to meet their needs" (Szirmai 2015, 7).

This definition and the framework expressed in the report "Our Common Future" recognizes the dependence of human beings on the environment to meet their needs. It suggests that environment and economy are becoming more intertwined. The report stresses that humanity depends on

the environment for security and basic existence. It emphasizes the need of the environment for the economy and the
well-being of people for now and for the future (Hopwood
2005, 38). Tatyana P. Soubbotina, a consultant at the World
Bank Institute, describes sustainable development in
this way:

> Sustainable development could probably be
> otherwise called "equitable and balanced", meaning
> that, in order for development to continue
> indefinitely, it should balance the interests of
> different groups of people within the same
> generation and among generations, and do so
> simultaneously in three major interrelated areas–
> economic, social, and environmental (Soubbotina
> 2004, 9).

Nature and Scope *of Sustainable Development*

Sustainable development attempts to balance the environmental, social, and economic limitations of a society.
Many throughout the world think that natural resources are
being carelessly used to meet the present need and if that
kind of misuse continues, natural resources will not last for
more than a few decades. Although many surmise that
sustainable development is relevant only in the environmental context, it is also relevant in economic, individual,
and social contexts. In fact, sustainable development theorists are concerned about social and economic development
without affecting the potential benefits for the future. They
concentrate on achieving economic and social well-being
for many human generations.

The   relationship   between   development   and

environment has given birth to the sustainable development concept. The central idea of sustainable development is that global ecosystems and humanity itself can be threatened by neglecting the environment. Environmental economists are concerned that the long-term neglect of environmental assets is likely to jeopardize the durability of economic growth. Sustainable development therefore "involves maximizing the net benefits of economic development, subject to maintaining the services and quality of natural resources over time." Its concern is about balancing the objectives of economic growth and attending to environmental considerations (Dang 2015, 14).

Recently, there has been an increase of interest in the field of sustainable development as people are mindful of the consequences of human actions on the environment.

It is an important shift in understanding relationships of humanity with nature and among people. And this shift is in contrast to the dominant view of the separation of environmental issues from socioeconomic issues for the past hundreds of years. The relationship between people and the environment was always considered as humanity's triumph over nature. It is the Promethean view, which claims that human knowledge and technology can help in overcoming all challenges, including the natural and environmental. According to Francis Bacon, one of the founders of modern science, "the world is made for man, not man for the world" (Hopwood 2005, 39). Thus, this view was linked with the development of capitalism, the industrial revolution and modern science.

There are natural limits to economic growth, because

the earth cannot support an ever-expanding economic growth as a result of industrialization. Since sustainable development protects the right of future generations to a high standard of living, it highlights the need for global equality and helps prevent a resource crisis for the future (Royal Geographical Society with IBG 2013). "There are three pillars of sustainable development: social, environmental and economic. All three must be present for a country to attain sustainable development" (Royal Geographical Society with IBG 2013).

Therefore, sustainable development theorists are committed to improve the quality of life in a comprehensive manner. As a result of economic, social, environmental and cultural integration, there will be sustainable development in future generations (Dang 2015, 14). In short, the scope of sustainable development covers a wide range from restoring the damage already done to the environment by earlier unsustainable patterns of economic growth, to follow a pattern of development that avoids further damage to the planet's ecosystem, and to ensure meeting the needs of the present as well as future generations.

Limitations of Sustainable Development

One of the criticisms of sustainable development is the fact that it could constrain the ability of developing nations to industrialize and experience rapid growth. It may also be difficult to implement universal and long-term policies for poor countries (Dang 2015, 14). One of the fundamental flaws of sustainable development is that it fails to meaningfully address the needs, values and cultural differences of the developing countries. Arturo Escobar argues that it is simply a new manifestation of an old discourse. Sustainable development theory simply redistributes and reshuffles neoliberal concerns of basic needs, population, resources, and technology. Another main criticism of sustainable development theory according to Hilary Hove is that:

> It unsuccessfully attempts to mesh two contradictory endeavors: environmental protection and economic expansion. Failing to reconcile this inconsistency, sustainable development avoids a serious criticism of the West's role in the underdevelopment and other global inequities, simply allowing for our continued growth without meaningful reform (Hove 2004, 51).

HUMAN DEVELOPMENT THEORY

Human development theory was introduced by the Indian Noble Laureate Professor Amartya Sen. He has made huge contributions to the development of this theory by defining development in terms of human freedom and capabilities. Sen argues that the goal of development is to develop human "capabilities." Thus, he promotes human well-being (quality of life) over mere economic growth, and proposes non-monetary aspects in measuring development. His measuring indicators include health, education, environment, and material well-being. He argues that economic development is necessary, but not in itself enough in terms of the quality of life (Dang 2015, 13).

In 1990, when the United Nations Development Program (UNDP) published the first Human Development Report (HDR), it changed the concept of development. Human development was defined as the progress toward human well-being. The HDR also published statistics of an extensive range of well-being indicators on a country-level. It offered both the measurement and comparison tools for the governments, NGOs, and researchers (Stanton 2007, 3).

A broader perspective of human development goals is reflected in the World Bank's Development Report, which includes "better education, higher standards of health and nutrition, less poverty, a cleaner environment, more equality of opportunity, greater individual freedom, and a richer cultural life" (Dang 2015, 13).

Since its inception human development theory has always been about creating environments for people to realize their potential as human beings, and to help them live life to the fullest. This idea of developing people is very close to what Jawaharlal Nehru, the first prime minister of independent India said in 1947, "Give every Indian the fullest opportunity to develop himself according to his capacity." He was referring to the tasks that lay ahead for the new country, and how the people will be able to develop themselves given the opportunity. Thus, opportunities are essential to allow every person to develop according to their own capacity, which will result in their well-being (Harriss 2014, 6).

Nature and Scope of Human Development Theory

According to the United Nations Development Program (UNDP), human development is a process of analyzing people's choices. These choices can be countless and they can change over time. But at all levels of development, there are three essential areas of development for people:

> The first is to lead a long and healthy life. The second is to acquire knowledge. And the third is to have access to resources needed for a decent standard of living. If these essential choices are not available, many other opportunities will be

unapproachable. However, human development does not end there. Other choices like political, economic and social freedom, self-respect and human rights are also inseparable parts of human development (Shah 2013-2015).

Human development is the process of broadening people's choices. The human development theory looks at income as a means, not as an end, to people's development (Shah 2013-2015).

Human development theory includes people in the development discourse. It focuses on increasing and widening people's choices and raising their levels of well-being. It includes various dimensions of human life such as economic, social, political, cultural, educational, physical and psychological. Advocates of human development theory argue that income is only one of the many components of development. And commodities are only of value to us in terms of what they allow us actually to do. The focus is on the freedom that a person actually has to do this or be that—things that he or she may value doing or being. Thus, both positive and negative freedoms are important aspects of human development theory (Harriss 2014, 36).

Advocates of human development theory believe that development cannot be achieved through economic improvement alone; it must be a combination of social, cultural, political and economic improvement where individuals have the freedom to make choices. Aside from financial assets, all human beings have livelihood assets. Financial assets include wages, savings, pensions and remittances. Human assets include education, knowledge, skills and health. Physical assets include transport, communications, technology and energy. Social assets include representatives, friends, neighbors and leaders. And natural assets include land, water, minerals and wildlife.

Theory proponents also emphasize the importance of what people can achieve with their resources. Development should be assessed on an individual scale and everyone should be equally entitled to a better life. Therefore, if human development is emphasized in the socioeconomic development of a country, the people would enjoy freedom and well-being (Royal Geographical Society with IBG 2013).

Limitations of Human Development Theory

Critics of the human development theory claim that the quality of data in the HDI is very poor. They say, "the census data used to calculate the HDI are unreliable because of the infrequency of census data collection, the possibility of inaccurate reporting, and a lack of complete coverage within countries" (Stanton 2007, 22). They also claim that the HDI calculation method is random and it cannot be justified. Another criticism is that there is redundancy in the HDI. Opponents suggest that the indicators in the HDI are interrelated, and the HDI does not offer any new information beyond what is already available in GDP per capita (Stanton 2007, 22).

One of major criticisms of human development theory is that there is no need for people to have freedom in order to live fulfilled lives. They can be satisfied with their life even without completely free choices. On the other hand, people can have free choices but still live in poverty. And others criticize human development theory with the claim that free choices can focus on individual needs, but not the needs of those of society or collective groups. Human capability alone does not necessarily produce development if societal changes are causing more vulnerability. Since the focus of development is on the individual human being, human development theory has the tendency to neglect other aspects of society that affect the individual and his/her development.

POST-DEVELOPMENT THEORY

Post-development theory is a result of postmodern critique of modernism theory. It has been greatly influenced by the work of Michel Foucault. Post-development theory attempts to deconstruct the concept of development in order to reveal the operations of power and knowledge in development discussion and development initiatives. Advocates of the theory reject the concept of development because it has become a reaction of the developed countries to the problem of poverty in developing countries.

Firstly, the traditional concept of development is Eurocentric because the West is considered "developed" while the rest of the world is perceived as "underdeveloped." Secondly, proponents argue that the traditional concept of development has authoritarian and technocratic implications. Development discourse is critiqued as based on Western ideas of progress and imposes those ideas on the underdeveloped countries. As a result, it suppresses the local cultures and interests (Kippler 2010, 1).

The history of post-development theory goes back to the roots of development practices that began after the World

War II. Development was understood as the intervention by giving aid to raise living standards, increase income, and provide better health for the poor. This sympathetic idea led to the rise of development industry comprised of institutions, processes, and discourses to help the underdeveloped nations. But that help was intended for the underdeveloped nations to follow the developed Western nations as models. One of the examples of such help is a global campaign called "Make Poverty History." It encouraged greater intervention by developed Western nations into the developing world. In response to such development intention, there was a rise of post-modern critiques against Western development plans, which paved the way for post-development theory (Ahorro 2008, 1). Thus, Post-development theory is not about identifying the most efficient way of delivering development; it is about questioning the very concept of development (Pieterse 2000, 175).

Post-development theory is fundamentally a reaction to the dilemmas, confusions, and frustrations with standard development practices. Proponents of post-development theory rejected standard development practices. According to Gilbert Rist, "It is the new religion of the West." And according to Constantino, "it means cultural Westernization and homogenization." Therefore, advocates of post-development rejected standard development practices not merely on account of its results but because of its intentions and worldviews (Pieterse 2000, 175). The first wave of post-development theory took its shape through the writings of scholars such as Escobar, Esteva, Kothari, Nandy and Rist. In his book, *Encountering Development: The Making and Unmaking of the Third World*, Arturo Escobar writes:

The process of unmaking development, however, is

slow and painful, and there are no easy solutions or prescriptions. From the West, it is much more difficult to perceive that development is at the same time self-destructing and being unmade by social action, even as it continues to destroy people and nature (Escobar 1995, 217).

In response to the first wave, there was a second wave of post-development theory, evident in the writings of Lind, Matthews, Nusted, Rapley and Ziai who widened the meaning of post-development. In his book, *Exploring Post Development: Theory and practice, problems and perspectives,* Ziai Aram writes, "When post-development writers reject development, they are opening up possibilities for other ways of understanding the society and the economy" (Ziai 2007, 201). This process of refinement has given post-development theory greater utility and opportunity for growth (Ahorro 2008, 1).

Nature and Scope of Post-Development Theory

The first wave of post-development theorists argued that development practices destroyed the diversity of social, cultural, economic, and political systems of the underdeveloped nations. And those systems were replaced with externally imposed homogenous models of the Western nations. A common thread found in this first wave of post-development theory is that it portrays development as West-centered, and advocates for new ways of thinking about non-Western countries (Ahorro 2008, 1).

In his 1995 edition of the book, *Encountering Development: The Making and Unmaking of the Third Word,* Arturo Escobar presented the idea of post development, which became quite controversial. He provides an assessment of post development in his 2012 edition of the same book, explaining how post development theory took shape as a critique of poststructuralist and postcolonial critique. He talks about three interrelated things that post development was meant to describe:

> "First, the need to decenter development; that is, to displace it from its centrality in representations and discussions about conditions in Asia, Africa, and Latin America. A corollary of this first goal was to open up the discursive space to other ways of describing those conditions, less mediated by the premises and experiences of "development." Second, in displacing development's centrality from the discursive imaginary, postdevelopment suggested that it was indeed possible to think about the end of development. In other words, it identified alternatives *to* development rather than development alternatives, as a concrete possibility. Third, postdevelopment emphasized the importance of transforming the "political economy of truth," that is, development's order of expert knowledge and power (Escobar 2012 Edition, xii-xiii)

Post-development theory proponents argue that poor people need to address their own problems using their own ideas and resources. Poor nations do not have to develop according to Western economic development models; instead, they should be empowered to create their own economic development models. They do not have to follow the cultural and moral guidance of western donors; instead they should preserve their cultural and moral values (Royal Geographical Society with IBG 2013).

Economist William Easterly gives examples of Hong Kong and Singapore to emphasize the locally initiated development models. Both former British colonies were poor, but by 2001 both Hong Kong and Singapore overtook their former colonial master. They neither received a significant amount of foreign aid nor any military assistance from Western countries. Their success was the result of their own ideas and initiatives (Easterly 2006, 348).

Limitations of Post-Development Theory

The main limitation of post-development theory is that it has been rooted primarily in the experiences of Latin America and Africa. However, the examples of economic success in select Asian countries is typically not discussed in order to conclusively assert that development does not work. Critics acknowledge post-development theory's ability to identify the problems of development theory and policy, but complain that it does not offer any concrete alternatives to solve the problem. And it does not provide practical alternatives to replace overseas assistance to the underdeveloped nations (Ahorro 2008, 1). Others have criticized post-development theory saying that the claims of post-development theorists are simply misleading and misrepresent the history of development. They claim that the attitude of post-development theorists towards existing development is narrow. Thus, "Post-development theory has also been characterized as 'beyond-development' and 'anti-development' for its disruption of development's reductive nature" (Ahorro 2008, 2).

As a result of analyzing and evaluating six key socioeconomic development theories, I have come to realize that no theory is perfect. All are focused on a particular area of development but not on holistic development. There is no theory that in and of itself holds the key to effective analysis of all economic problems and changes in the world. Some of the theories may work very well in developing certain aspects of the lives of the poor, but they are not enough for their holistic development. Therefore, I would like to propose holistic development as the framework to explain poverty and to respond to it. A holistic development framework proposes an integrated development of economic, psychological, social, and spiritual aspects so that poor people will experience shalom.

4

HOLISTIC DEVELOPMENT FRAMEWORK

Holistic development is an approach to measuring activity by taking into account not only economic development, but also its social, psychological, and spiritual aspects. It is the intentional integration of economic, psychological, social, and spiritual response to poverty for the holistic development of the poor. It is birthed out of analyzing and critiquing six key socioeconomic theories, all of which are focused on a particular aspect of development (e.g. economic well-being and human well-being). None of these six theories, however, focuses on the holistic development of people, especially that of the poor.

The United Nations has been using the phrase "holistic approach" in terms of its development efforts that primarily focus on happiness and well-being. It has adapted this idea from the human development theory (based on Amartya Sen's Human Development Index) and the sustainable development theory (based on the Burntland Report). It is a positive sign that the concept of holistic development is being used in various sectors. However, those sectors tend to remove the spiritual aspect of development, a facet that is essential for the holistic development of a person.

The concept of shalom in the context of the proposed components of holistic development is not new in Christian literature. Ruth Callanta, the founder of Center for Community Transformation (CCT) talks about the need for development to be integrated and holistic in her chapter, "A Transformational Strategy: Toward Filling the Hungry with Good Things", in the book *The Church and Poverty in Asia*. She discusses the physical, social and economic needs of human beings, and the need for development in all these dimensions. Spiritual, physical, economic, and social needs must be addressed in order to build up a whole person. Though she is absolutely right about the need for development to be integrated and holistic, she does not include psychological needs of the poor (Wanak 2008, 150).

Thus, a holistic development framework is proposed to measure the effectiveness of evangelical Christian response to poverty, and its impact on economic, psychological, social, and spiritual development of the poor.

Holistic Development Framework

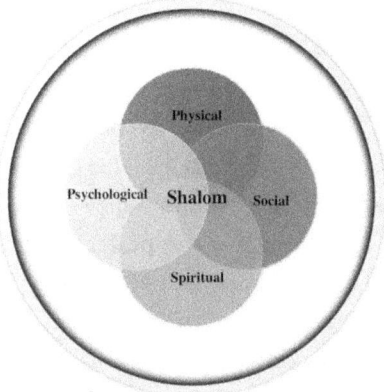

Different Kinds of Poverty

i. Economic Poverty

ii. Psychological Poverty

iii. Social Poverty

iv. Spiritual Poverty

Shalom: The Goal of Holistic Development

i. Concept of Shalom in the Bible

ii. Scope of Shalom

iii. Moving Towards Shalom

THE CONCEPT of holistic development framework integrating the economic, psychological, social, and spiritual components is adapted most specifically from Bryant Myers's definition of poverty and Bob Moffitt's definition of development. Myers, in his book, *Walking with the Poor*, says, "Poverty is the result of relationships that do not work, that are not just, that are not for life, that are not harmonious or enjoyable. Poverty is the absence of shalom in all its meanings" (Myers 2011, 141).

Moffett talks about physical, social, psychological, and

spiritual development. He quotes Luke 2:52 as a clear presentation of a biblical view of human development: "And Jesus grew in wisdom and stature, and in favor with God and men." This passage refers to the development of Jesus. Jesus himself grew in wisdom. He also grew physically, spiritually, and socially. Christians believe that Jesus was the perfect man and, therefore, the perfect model. His development can serve as a model for people. It is important to see that Jesus achieved His full human potential in these four areas of life in the context of relative material poverty (Moffitt 2007, 6-7).

The holistic development framework proposed in this research is an integration of economic, psychological, social, and spiritual development of the poor with the goal for them to experience shalom as a result. Poverty therein is defined in economic, psychological, social, and spiritual terms and evangelical Christians in the Philippines are urged to respond to all of them in an integrated manner. As these four kinds of poverty are interrelated with each other, the response needs to be integrated as well, which involves economic, psychological, social, and spiritual development of the poor.

DIFFERENT KINDS OF POVERTY

People usually understand poverty as primarily an economic condition. It is the state of not having enough money to buy basic necessities. While this is certainly one aspect of poverty, it does not capture its full significance and scope. There are also other kinds of poverty that people are facing today. This research will look at four different kinds: economic poverty, psychological poverty, social poverty, and spiritual poverty.

ECONOMIC POVERTY

Though poverty is a complex and multidimensional phenomenon, it is usually defined in economic terms. People are poor because they lack the resources to get the things they need. Economic poverty is the lack of basic necessities for material well-being. Some of these basic needs are food, clothing, housing, clean water, land, and other assets. Encyclopedia Britannica defines poverty as:

> The state of one who lacks a usual or socially acceptable amount of money or material possessions. Poverty is said to exist when people lack the means to satisfy their basic needs. In this context, the identification of poor people first requires a determination of what constitutes basic needs. These may be defined as narrowly as "those necessary for survival" or as broadly as "those reflecting the prevailing standard of living in the community (Encyclopedia Britannica: "Poverty," 2011).

The most common definition of poverty comes from the World Bank, which relates to the economic poverty. According to the World Bank, poverty is a situation where a person is living below the income of $3.10 per day, and extreme poverty is a situation where a person is living below the income of $1.90 per day. The World Bank comes up with these figures based on the average poverty line in the world's 15 poorest countries (World Bank 2015). Economic poverty usually affects the psychological, social, and spiritual aspects of a person.

PSYCHOLOGICAL POVERTY

Johan Janse van Rensburg, in his article "The Psychology of Poverty" says, "When investigating the phenomenon of poverty, the question is not only why people are poor, but also, and most importantly, why people remain poor. Why is it that poverty seems to keep people in some kind of psychological bondage from which they are unable to escape?" (Rensburg 2013, 1). Psychological poverty is the state of having an unhealthy and poor frame of mind. It reduces the confidence of people in themselves.

Psychological poverty is a disease that a great number of people are suffering from today. It also creates a poverty mentality in people who tend to believe that they are poor and that they will remain poor. People are literally losing their minds in their psychological warfare with poverty. This mindset has a long history that goes back thousands of years and is strongly rooted in the minds of the psychologically poor. It cannot be blamed on an economic downturn, and it cannot be solved overnight. Psychological poverty is usually self-inflicted. If a person has a poverty mindset, then he is the only person who can pull himself out of it (Parker 2010-2012).

A study done by Warwick University has claimed that poverty has a significant negative effect on cognitive ability. It is equal to losing a full night of sleep. Mental poverty hinders the ability to make positive choices and shackles the poor to an endless cycle of poverty. Dr. Anandi Mani, professor at Warwick University, shows that it is the flaw of poverty, not the poor, that creates the poverty trap. He says, "The poor, in this view, are less capable not because of inherent traits, but because the very context of poverty imposes load and impedes cognitive capacity. The findings, in other words, are not about poor people, but about any people who find themselves poor" (Mani et al 2013, 980).

SOCIAL POVERTY

Social poverty is also understood as relational poverty. It can affect anyone regardless of race, gender, age, or socioeconomic status. It is a form of poverty far more destructive than economic poverty. Relational poverty is a deep lack of the connectedness with others that people need for their well-being. People are turning to virtual communications more than face-to-face interactions, but even the most advanced communication technology cannot close the gap of relational distance (Szalavitz and Perry 2010, 292). That is why Bryant Myers proposes that poverty is primarily relational and that its cause is predominantly spiritual. He then goes on to say,

> The poor are poor largely because they live in networks of relationships that do not work for their well-being. Their relationships with others are often oppressive and disempowering as a result of the non-poor "playing god" in the lives of the poor. Their relationship within themselves is diminished and debilitated as a result of the grind of poverty and the

feeling of permanent powerlessness. Their relationship with those they call "others" is experienced as exclusion. Their relation with their environment is increasingly less productive because poverty leaves no room for caring for the environment. Their relationship with the God who created them and sustains their life is distorted by an inadequate knowledge of who God is and what God wishes for all humankind (Myers 2011, 787).

Globalization and labor markets have made social poverty a common experience of people in developing countries, including the Philippines. According to the data from the Philippine Overseas Employment Administration, there are approximately 9.5 to 12.5 million Filipinos working in other countries, which is around 10-11% of the total population of the nation (POEA 2013). They are usually called Overseas Filipino Workers (OFW). OFWs have scattered throughout various countries and cities for better opportunities. This creates loneliness, marital problems, parenting issues, identity crises and other social problems in the Philippine society. Though remittances from OFWs play a vital role in sustaining the Philippine economy, they create social poverty in the long run.

Social poverty also involves social exclusion, which is being excluded from social, economic, cultural, political arenas. In her chapter "The concept and measurement of social exclusion" Ruth Levitas defines social exclusion in this way:

Social exclusion is a complex and multi-dimensional process. It involves the lack or denial of resources, rights, goods and services, and the inability to participate in the normal relationships and activities, available to the majority of people in a society, whether in economic, social, cultural or political arenas. It affects both the quality of life of individuals and the equity and cohesion of society as a whole (Levitas, R. A. 2006, 123).

SPIRITUAL POVERTY

On the subject of spiritual poverty, Matthew 5:3 is a passage that usually comes up. It is one of the few verses in the New Testament that seems to provide a definitive statement on poverty by Jesus himself. Despite this, many people have wrestled with what being poor in spirit really means. According to BDAG, when he said, "Blessed are the poor in spirit, for theirs is the kingdom of heaven," the Greek word, *ptōchoi* "poor" in this context implies "lacking in spiritual worth" (Danker 2000, 896). Jesus called this a "blessed" condition because it helps people to draw closer to God. According to Johannes Baptist Metz,

> It is we human beings bearing witness to ourselves, professing loyalty to our radical poverty, and shouldering the weight of self-emptying. It is our consent of self-surrender. In poverty of spirit we learn to accept ourselves as beings who do not belong to ourselves. (Metz 1998, 31).

Spiritual poverty is the state of incompleteness before

God. When people experience neediness, incompleteness, and dependency, they often become overwhelmed. Thus, spiritual poverty is the cure for narcissism, self-right-eousness, and other problems human beings face. When people see their brokenness, they do not feel better about themselves; instead, they feel that something is terribly wrong within themselves. In fact, it does not matter whether they have problems or struggles in life or not; they still need God. People need God's grace and mercy. However, not everyone is aware of his or her neediness. For those who are aware of their neediness, Jesus described them as "poor in spirit." That is why Anne Bradley and Art Lindsley say, "the issue is not poverty per se, but rather the attitude of humility and reliance on God that it can produce in us. That's why Matthew's version of the beatitude isn't just "'Blessed are the poor,' but 'Blessed are the poor in spirit'" (Bradley and Lindsley 2014, 18).

SHALOM: THE GOAL OF HOLISTIC DEVELOPMENT

Shalom is the ultimate goal of holistic development. When evangelical Christians respond to poverty physically, psychologically, socially, and spiritually, poor people will experience shalom. These four aspects are interconnected and they affect each other. If the response to poverty is only economic, other aspects of development will not achieve their full potentials. Likewise, if the response to poverty is only focused on the psychological, social and spiritual aspects, economic development will not achieve its full potential. Thus, intentional and integrated response to all four areas is essential for the poor to experience shalom.

CONCEPT OF SHALOM

What comes to mind when the word shalom is spoken? Is it absence of war, a sense of calm, an absence of conflict? Shalom is a beautiful classical Hebrew word, transliterated as šālôm. The triliteral root it derives from, ŠLM, means variously in its different verbal stems, "to be completed, ready... to remain healthy, unharmed...to keep peace...make restitution...to recompense, reward to restore...to finish...to deliver up...to be at peace" (HALOT, vol 4, 1532–33).

Jewish people usually greet each other with the word "shalom" to wish peace, prosperity, completeness and welfare. According to William D. Bjoraker, an associate professor of Judeo Christian Studies and Contemporary Western Culture at William Carey International University, "shalom is an idea, a value, a condition that has long resonated deep within the heart and soul of the Jewish people. The ardent longing for shalom is expressed repeatedly in their songs, national traditions, and liturgies" (Bjoraker, 2012).

The word "shalom" is usually translated as "peace" in English. But translating shalom into one word alone will not give the full depth and richness of its meaning. There is no English word that can effectively convey the depth behind the concept of shalom in the Bible. Understanding the scope of this word is very important to better understand its concept and meaning.

SCOPE OF SHALOM

Stephen D. Jones, in his book, *Peaceteacher: Jesus' Way of Shalom,* argues that the scope of shalom is holistic. It is certainly more than nonviolence or cessation of hostilities. Translating shalom into the word "peace" fails to capture its fuller meaning in the original Hebrew language. Shalom certainly includes an absence of war and commitment to nonviolence, but it is more than that. "It is the inner wholeness of the fulfilled person. It is also a relational word including (upward) peace with God, and (outward) peaceful integration within the society of God's people" (Dom-Nwachukwu and Lee 2014, 112). Thus, the scope of shalom is to seek the well-being of everyone.

Shalom embraces justice and peace with oneself, with others, and with God and his creation. It has to do with living God's way with oneself, with others, and with his creation. When Jesus spoke of peace, whether in Greek, the language of the NT, or Aramaic, the language he likely spoke, he likely meant the semantic range of the classical Hebrew word shalom. The English word, peace, arises out of dualistic thinking (inner peace and outer peace) which limits its scope. You can either be an obsessed peacemaker or you can be a self-absorbed peace-seeker. Since the concept of the English word peace is limited to a dualistic sense, it cannot explain the comprehensive meaning of shalom, which is more holistic. It means wellbeing, wholeness, and its scope is the well-being of everyone and everything (Jones 2007, 7-8, 15).

MOVING TOWARDS SHALOM

God's work in the world, *Missio Dei,* is actually the work of shalom. God did not just create the world and abandon it. He is continually at work in the world that he created. And according to Richard Stearns, "God leaves us here because he has a mission for us to fulfill" (Stearns 2014, 5). God's desire is to ensure that his creation is respected, nurtured and enjoyed. That is why his work in the world, *Missio Dei,* is about creating and sustaining shalom, as well as restoring it when it is absent among people. Since shalom is the mission of God, it should also be the mission of God's people (Gruchy 2004, 1-2). But before moving toward that mission, it is important to know why Christians are working on it.

Since the goal of shalom is to establish well-being within an individual, society or community, it requires right relationships with others. People can obtain that picture of right relationships when they connect shalom with justice. These two words are closely related to each other and are often found in parallel lines in the Old Testament. Though shalom is more than justice, it produces a just society. Likewise, shalom and covenant are also closely related to each other. When connected together, it indicates that shalom comes as a result of God's covenantal commitment to his people. And, God's intentions for his covenant people will help bring an understanding of their mission in God's vision of shalom (Brown 2003, 1).

God's plan is to restore wholeness and healing to all areas of brokenness that affects all of his creation. His original creation was whole, complete and perfect. But, that original wholeness was broken by the fall of man. God did not want his creation to remain in that state. He initiated restoration by sending of his son, Jesus Christ, to the world. The work of Jesus reconciles sinners to God and establishes shalom in the world. And that shalom encompasses all dimensions of human life: spiritual, physical, mental and relational (Gruchy 2004, 3).

The Old Testament makes it clear that shalom does not come through the protection of military power, the accumulation of wealth, the exploitation of people, the use of medical knowledge, or even through religious observances. Rather, shalom comes through trusting in God in all areas of life, and that was the model of life God designed for the nation of Israel. In the New Testament Jesus told His disciples not to worry about what to eat and what to wear because life is more than food and clothing. He also told them to sell their possessions and give to the poor in order to have treasures in heaven. Jesus knew that their hearts would always be on their possessions.

In other words, if people depend on their wealth, knowledge, and military might to experience shalom, their hopes will be based on the false shalom values of this world. God established the covenant with the children of Israel to affect their social and economic structures so they could experience shalom. And, this is why Jesus set new ethical, spiritual, and social standards for his followers in order for them to experience the same. So, moving toward shalom, people are to live and work according to God's command and his covenant to establish God's new shalom kingdom (Sine 2006, 5).

Since shalom is the way of God in the world, people are to embrace one another as God has embraced them with His love and grace. As shalom is the experience of right relationships with all creation, the church, being the sign of the coming kingdom, should be a welcoming and inclusive community. The church should be especially welcoming and inclusive to the poor, as God has a particular concern for the poor. Millions suffer in the absence of shalom, and the church should be able to provide an avenue for them to experience the presence of shalom. Therefore, moving towards shalom, the church should be faithful to the 'Missio Dei' by being an agent of shalom to the community (Gruchy 2004, 3-4). That is why Richard Stearns claims that God requires of us much more than just having a personal and transforming relationship with Him. He wants people to have a public and transforming relationship with the world around them (Stearns 2014, 2).

Shalom is about relationships. It embraces all the dimensions of relationships that contribute to the wholeness God intends for people's lives. In the creation story, there are glimpses of God's intention for humanity. His mission in this fallen and broken world is reconciliation. And his mission of reconciliation is holistic, including relationships with God, self, others, and rest of God's creation. Thus, reconciliation begins with God and leads people to experience shalom by transforming personal, social, and structural dimensions of life (Katongole and Rice. Eds. 2008, 142).

This mission has never changed from the fall to the new creation in Christ, to its fulfillment in the coming of Jesus. Therefore, at the heart of shalom is the relationship of people with God. But it does not stop there. The wholeness of shalom is also about the relationships people share with one another. God did not create humans to live as isolated individuals, but to live in harmony with others including the rest of God's creation (Sine 2006, 7).

5

EVANGELICAL CHRISTIAN RESPONSE TO POVERTY

E vangelical Christians are visible in addressing the problem of poverty around the world, including the Philippines. There are varieties of the programs and services that evangelical Christian churches, NGOs, and INGOs offer in addressing poverty in the country. This chapter will try to explore their understanding of poverty and their involvement in addressing the problem of poverty in the Philippines. Then Evangelical Christian response to poverty is evaluated based on the Holistic Development Framework which includes economic, psychological, social, and spiritual development of the poor.

UNDERSTANDING POVERTY AND ITS CAUSES

Poverty is primarily a lack of material things. All evangelical Christian leaders interviewed defined poverty mainly in economic terms. They explained poverty as a lack of basic needs (food, shelter, and clothing) and a lack of basic services (education, healthcare, and clean water). Poverty is understood as an economic condition where services and other needs are lacking. Underdevelopment, malnourishment, hunger, and lack of education are forms of poverty.

Half of the evangelical Christian leaders interviewed defined poverty in spiritual terms in addition to their economic definition. They described poverty as spiritual brokenness. It is a result of broken relationship with God. Poverty is never God's intention. It is the consequence of sin. The implication of this definition could possibly be that only people without right relationship with God are poor. It could also imply that Christians should not be poor as it is not God's intention. Poverty is also defined as a result of the fallen state of man. It falls right into the agenda of Satan. A lie is at the core of poverty that Satan uses daily to spread cruel and destructive message. Poverty is presumed to be a reality of the fallenness of man and there is nothing much that can be done about it. Spiritual definitions of poverty reveal the reality that poverty is the result of human sinfulness.

Some evangelical Christian leaders defined poverty in psychological terms in addition to their economic and spiritual definitions. They understand poverty as powerlessness. One of them explained powerlessness as, "no access to productive assets, no access to institution services, and no ability to influence decisions that affect their lives." They believe that powerlessness results in the poor becoming even poorer while the rich are getting richer. It was interesting that none of the evangelical Christian leaders mentioned the social aspect of poverty. All of them defined poverty in economic, spiritual, and psychological terms but not in social terms. It is apparent that very few evangelical Christian leaders realize the psychological needs and none of them realize the social needs of the poor. It is presumed that their programs and services to respond to poverty focus primarily on the economic and spiritual aspects of poverty.

It is evident that poverty is persistent in the Philippines. What then keeps poverty persistent? Knowing the reasons behind the persistence of poverty is necessary for evangelical Christian leaders. It will help them to focus their poverty alleviation efforts on the things that keep poverty persistent in the Philippines. When asked about the causes of poverty, all the evangelical Christian leaders interviewed mentioned the corrupt and unjust political system as a common cause of poverty. Moreover, seventy percent of them said that the corrupt and unjust political system is also the main reason why poverty is persistent in the Philippines. They mentioned that government structures and policies are not favorable to the poor. They widen the gap between the rich and the poor in the country. The unjust political system keeps poverty persistent as it is favorable to the rich. It is agreed that corruption is evident in almost all levels of the government. Twenty percent of them talked about price increase in basic commodities and the constant struggle of farmers adds to the persistence of poverty. They seem to be concerned by the fact that government plans and policies are not favorable to the poor but are favorable to the rich and powerful.

Some of them referred to recurring natural disaster as one of the major causes of poverty in the Philippines. The Philippines is prone to natural disasters where at least a few disasters occur every year. Some of the frequent natural disasters that affect the Philippine islands are typhoons, floods, earthquakes, and volcanic activity. They are very frequent because of the country's geographical location in the Pacific Ring of Fire. None of the evangelical Christian leaders referred to population growth as one of the causes of persistent poverty in the Philippines, though existing research data shows that population growth is one of the key causes.

ADDRESSING POVERTY

Since evangelical Christians in the Philippines are visible in addressing the problem of poverty, I asked the interviewees, "How is your church, NGO or INGO addressing the problem of poverty?" In response, all of the evangelical Christian leaders mentioned about their programs and services to provide the basic needs of the poor. Their main programs and services are: feeding programs, medical missions, giving scholarships, providing school supplies, and alternative learning systems. It is apparent that most of the evangelical Christian churches, NGOs, and INGOs interviewed are responding to poverty by providing immediate needs of the poor.

Majority of them said that they respond to poverty by providing educational programs and services to the poor. They talked about Alternative Learning System (ALS), vocational training, and livelihood programs to help the poor. They are designed for mostly out-of-school youth as well as adults and geared towards jobs. It is presumed that the majority of evangelical Christians are investing in the education of the youth who come from poor families. One of the evangelical Christian leaders is empowering these next-generation leaders from poverty by teaching music. They seem to believe that there is hope in education.

Many evangelical Christian leaders mentioned programs and services that are designed to nurture the poor spiritually. They are upfront in their spiritual programs and services and mention it even before they begin their work. Their spiritual activities include Bible studies, values formation classes, prayers, and visitations. The other half said that they integrate spiritual activities in all of their programs and services. One of the leaders mentioned the importance of responding to poverty by teaching and preaching about poverty in evangelical Christian churches in order to mobilize people for poverty alleviation efforts. It is presumed that, in one way or another, all evangelical Christian churches, NGOs, and INGOs interviewed are addressing poverty by meeting the spiritual needs of the poor.

Some of the evangelical Christian leaders talked about disaster risk reduction and emergency response as one of their primary responses to poverty. It is a response that requires skills and manpower. They respond to natural calamities to provide immediate humanitarian aid, and they also provide disaster risk reduction training in natural disaster-prone areas in the country. It seems the majority of the INGOs are involved in immediate disaster response and ongoing disaster risk reduction training. It seems to be one of their primary focuses as INGOs serving in a disaster-prone country. Besides, they have the resources, skills, and experience in providing such services.

Only a few leaders mentioned about a holistic approach to poverty alleviation. One of them shared their microfinance, discipleship, and livelihood programs in addressing both physical and spiritual needs of the poor. It is presumed that they are responding to the felt need and the real needs of the poor through their programs and services. They explained their holistic approach in terms of focusing on the head, heart, and the hands of the poor which is somewhat similar to the framework of this research. However, the head, heart and, hands analogy does not include the social aspect of poverty.

BIBLICAL SOLUTION TO POVERTY

Since the interviewees are some of the key leaders of evangelical Christian churches, NGOs, and INGOs, their views on a biblical solution to poverty are valuable for the study. Moreover, their views on the biblical solution to poverty form the basis of their response to poverty. All the evangelical Christian leaders interviewed mentioned that a relationship with God is the primary biblical solution to the problem of poverty. God is the solution to all problems and that includes poverty. They further added that the problem of poverty cannot be fully solved unless people are reconciled with God. This understanding has led them to put God as the foundation in responding to poverty and to include spiritual programs and services in their poverty alleviation efforts. Thirty-three percent of them talked about the need to share Christ with poor people to align them back to God. On the other hand, twenty-two percent shared about helping the poor find hope and right perspective in life as a result of their response to poverty.

Many of them said that proclamation and demonstration must go hand-in-hand. They seemed to allude to the idea of a coin that has Good News on one side and good work on the other. The biblical response to poverty is both spiritual and physical. It is presumed that evangelical Christians are to do good work and share the Good News without separating the two. They said that Jesus' ministry was full of feeding, healing, caring, saving, forgiving and associating with the poor and sinners. Therefore, it is necessary to present both physical and spiritual help to meet the needs of the poor.

One of the leaders quoted the Great Commandment passage from the Bible and suggested that loving God must result in loving the poor. If we say we love God, but we do not love poor people around us, then we do not really love God. Loving the poor should also result in sharing with them. If we say we love the poor but we do not share our resources for their need, then we do not really love them. Another leader pointed out that responding to poverty is not just giving things; it is about giving care and support for another human being. Poor people are also created in the image of God and they deserve our love, care, and compassion. It is presumed that Christian love must be expressed at all times in responding to the needs of the poor.

HOLISTIC RESPONSE TO POVERTY

Based on the holistic development framework that I have proposed in this book, holistic response is an integrated response to the economic, psychological, social, and spiritual poverty. Only one third of the evangelical Christian leaders think that there needs to be better collaboration among the evangelical Christians in responding to poverty. Instead of many churches doing small projects, they can join hands in order to help a poor community in a significant way. One of them also pointed out the need for an umbrella body of evangelical churches, NGOs, and INGOs in responding to poverty. They all seem to echo the lack of evangelical Christian individuals', churches', NGOs' and INGOs' effort to come together to create a poverty-response plan and implement it by using their unique skills, manpower, and resources. One of the leaders said, "Evangelical churches should recognize their role as a church and should not try to become NGOs/INGOs."

Some of them alluded to the idea that helping the poor and empowering the poor should be coordinated with the local churches. Since the church is based in the community, it should be the center from where we should respond to poor. It also helps the church to realize its role in poverty alleviation. Aside from that, it could also help the local churches to establish partnerships NGOs and INGOs. That kind partnership among evangelical Christians is necessary for better advocacy on behalf of the poor. It is presumed that NGOs and INGOs do not always coordinate with local churches in implementing their programs and services in the community.

It was interesting that all the evangelical Christian leaders had varied responses on holistic response to poverty, aside from the one above to which thirty percent of them agreed. There seems to be no consensus in terms of a particular approach aside from collaboration. It shows the reality of each individual church, NGO, and INGO doing their own thing without joining hands with others in responding to poverty. It is presumed that their programs and services are working well in helping the poor, but proper collaboration would definitely add strength to those individual efforts to respond to the economic, psychological, social, and spiritual development of the poor.

6

IMPACT OF EVANGELICAL CHRISTIAN RESPONSE TO POVERTY

There is no doubt that evangelical Christian response to poverty is making an impact in the lives of poor people in Metro Manila. In this chapter, I will highlight poor people's assessment of the evangelical Christian response to poverty in terms of their holistic development. The key findings from their assessment will be presented in light of the holistic development framework which includes economic, psychological, social, and spiritual development of the poor.

ECONOMIC DEVELOPMENT OF
THE POOR

"At its most basic level, economic development is the process though which a community creates material wealth and uses it to improve the well-being of its members" (Giugale 2014, 1). About half of all people who participated in focus group discussions conducted in the slums of Metro Manila mentioned that they have had significant economic development as a result of programs and services offered by evangelical Christian churches, NGOs, and INGOs. One of them said, "Before we used to borrow from '5-6 people' (Indian nationals who work as Loan Sharks). If we borrow 2,000 pesos, we would have to pay 2,400 pesos in a week." The person is a beneficiary of an NGO that provides loans for them with a very minimal interest rate to start a business, to provide education for their children, to build a house, and so on. It is evident that their financial situation has become better. The reason behind their significant economic growth is because of the financial training and seminars done by evangelical churches, NGOs, and INGOs. Most of the members whose economic situation has become better have been receiving programs and services for more than five years.

It was encouraging to hear about the financial awareness they have had as a result of programs and services conducted by evangelical Christians in their community. They have learned to "save for emergencies, buy necessary things only, spend wisely and share with others who don't have." These are valuable lessons in terms of handling money. It is apparent that they will apply it when they already have money with them. Some of them who are working part-time jobs shared about their experience of being careful in saving for their future. Most participants consider the programs and services that deal with the physical aspect of poverty were the most helpful for them in their current situation. The reason behind their significant economic growth is the emphasis of evangelical Christian churches, NGOs, and INGOs on their economic development. Aside from giving out used clothes, feeding programs, medical clinics and other immediate financial assistance evangelical Christians are working for the sustainable economic development of the poor. Community managed savings and credit association, vocational training, savings and credit cooperative, employment opportunities, and scholarships are some of the examples of programs and services that are making a significant impact on the economic development of the poor.

Economic development is indeed the most significant area of development that is evident in the lives of the poor people. Based on interviews with evangelical Christian leaders, economic development is the top priority of their programs and services to the poor. While some programs and services are just meeting the immediate needs of the poor, many are focused on long-term economic develop-

ment. Evangelical Christians emphasize economic development because of their understanding of poverty, which is
mainly lack of basic needs and services. Poor people share
the same understanding of poverty. That is why, evangelical
Christian churches, NGOs, and INGOs are intentional
about economic development, and the poor people are
appreciative of it. However, "it should not be surprising that
the solution to poverty must be complex" (Grudem and
Asmus 2013, 30).

PSYCHOLOGICAL DEVELOPMENT OF THE POOR

Almost all the participants of the focus group discussions I conducted in various poor communities talked about their significant psychological development as a result of programs and services offered by evangelical Christian churches, NGOs, and INGOs. One third of them talked about the change in their perspective in life and hope for their future. They are learning to let go of their "once poor, always poor" mindset. Majority of them were giving their responses and sharing their opinions, which in itself is a proof that their psychological situation has changed. Thus, many times, giving voice to the poor is the most helpful thing to do for the psychological development of the poor.

In many poor communities, there is considerable diversity in terms of ethnicity, race, gender, age, religion, and socioeconomic status. Hence, it is important to make sure that each group has meaningful participation both because each group may bring unique perspective and because participation is an important goal in its own right (Corbett and Fikkert 2015, 140).

Some of the poor people said, "We have our own identity now." They were referring to running their own businesses and making money compared to being dependent on their husbands for everything. One of the woman commented, "Before we were just housewives; now we are small business owners." It is evident from their sharing that evangelical Christian response is not always about just giving them fish but also teaching them how to fish. The mindset of the poor people seems to have changed and they seem to feel empowered as a result of the programs and services offered by evangelical Christian churches, NGOs, and INGOs.

Many of them appreciated the opportunities and avenues provided by evangelical Christian churches, NGOs, and INGOs. It has given them confidence and exposure to the world outside of their current poverty situation. They come from very poor family backgrounds and majority of them have a poverty mindset. Many of them still carry their poverty mindset, but they seem to be empowered to see beyond their current situation. They seem to be developing a positive outlook in life. They are trying to focus on their future rather than being discouraged by the realities of their present. They are determined to succeed. The programs and services of evangelical Christian churches, NGOs, and INGOs seem to have made a positive psychological impact on the poor people.

There were a few participants who have only experienced some psychological development who were mostly new members in the programs and services. Though many poor people shared about their psychological development experience as a result of programs and services offered by evangelical Christian churches, NGOs, and INGOs, it does not seem to be an intentional priority based on the interviews with the evangelical Christian leaders. It is presumed that psychological development is the result of programs and services that were intended for economic development. It is good that psychological development is taking place in the lives of the poor, even though it is not an intentional emphasis of the evangelical Christian response to poverty.

SOCIAL DEVELOPMENT OF THE POOR

Many poor people I talked to shared about their social development as a result of programs and services of evangelical Christian churches, NGOs, and INGOs. They mentioned how they have been able to get to know each other and share their journey to help each other grow through the weekly gatherings, worship services and small groups. Some of them said that they have new friends and more time to bond with each other. It has also been a place where they worship God and fellowship with each other.

Aside from finding new friends, they have also found friends in their communities as people see changes in their lives. One of them said, "I am elected as the president of women's group in my community." It shows that people are relational being and they need relationships with each other for their development. That is why Leroy Barber, who is dedicated to eradicating poverty, confronting homelessness, restoring local neighborhoods, and healing racism, writes about the importance of relationships:

We humans - made and female - are made in the

image of that triune God. And while the *imago Dei* in us has many aspects, it's clear that we are relational beings. We were created out of relationships and for relationship; we're relational at our core. We cannot help but function in community, and when we're not in community, we suffer consequences. We were made to be together, and that's by God's design. Human flourishing requires that we establish, mend, and maintain relationships with other people (Barber 2016, 570).

Some of them also talked about their good relationship with their family and friends at school resulting from the values they have learned. They have learned to be disciplined and work hard. It is evident that they have found good company to be with and a good environment to learn good habits. One of the young participants said, "If we were not here (in one of the NGOs), we would be with other friends doing drugs or playing video games." Through the programs and services of evangelical Christians, they have found a place where they can belong with one another.

Though some poor people talked about their social development as a result of the evangelical Christian response to poverty, it is not an area of emphasis for evangelical Christians based on interviews with them. None of the evangelical Christians leaders explained poverty in social terms. That is plausibly why they are also not intentional about the social development of the poor. However, social development has resulted from the spiritual programs and services of evangelical Christian churches, NGOs, and INGOs.

SPIRITUAL DEVELOPMENT OF
THE POOR

Almost all of the focus group discussion participants said they have experienced significant spiritual development as a result of programs and services of evangelical Christian churches, NGOs, and INGOs. Some of them have learned to pray and to do devotions at home. Others have also learned to put their faith into action. One of them said, "Faith without work is dead." Almost all of them said that they have grown spiritually since they started receiving programs and services by evangelical Christians. They mentioned about the habit of prayer and reading of God's word that they have learned. They all go to local churches every Sunday and are involved in church activities. It is apparent that many of them have been a good testimony to the people around them. That is the kind of development Steve Corbett and Brian Fikkert talks about, "Development is a process of ongoing change in which people move close to being in right relationship with God, self, others, and the rest of creation" (Corbett and Fikkert 2015, 207).

They learn about God, about God's love for them, and about hope in God. They enjoy fellowships, small group meetings, and worship services where they learn about God and His word. Those who have not accepted Jesus in their lives yet are still finding out more about God. These poor people seem sincere in their spiritual growth. Their willingness to learn and grow is genuine. They seem to be spiritually hungry and, in turn, they have been well fed by the evangelical Christian churches, NGOs, and INGOs.

Many of them are either new Christians who just came to know God or non-Christians who are still seeking God. It is evident from interviews with evangelical Christian leaders that spiritual development is the ultimate goal of their response to poverty. In many cases, spiritual development is subtle compared to economic development but is very intentional. Spiritual development is taking place in the lives of the poor as a result of Bible study, fellowship, prayer meeting, follow-up and so on done by evangelical Christians. It is perceived as the real solution to economic poverty; therefore, it is emphasized in the evangelical Christian response to poverty.

7

WHY IS POVERTY STILL PERSISTENT?

I t is evident that poverty is persistent in the Philippines. What then keeps poverty persistent? Knowing the reasons behind the persistence of poverty is necessary for evangelical Christian leaders. It will help them to focus their poverty alleviation efforts on the things that keep poverty persistent in the Philippines. Based on the findings of my research, the evangelical Christian churches, NGOs, and INGOs as represented by those interviewed, are seemingly having a positive impact in the holistic development of the poor in the country. Though economic and spiritual development of the poor seem to be the top priority of those interviewed, their programs and services are also making psychological and social impact in the lives of the poor. Since economic and spiritual poverty is more visible compared to psychological and social poverty, those are two apparent areas where evangelical Christians seem to focus their response on.

However, psychological and social development are equally important areas where the poor need development.

In fact, these are even more important because they affect the economic and spiritual development of the poor. Violeta Villaroman-Bautista argues that holistic development of the poor requires more than just meeting their physical needs. She highlights the need for evangelical Christians in the Philippines to respond to the psychological needs of the poor. She writes:

> The programs that target the care and development of the person, of relationships, of families – those we refer to as psychological programs – are important components of community work. They serve as intervening variables that enhance or contribute to the stabilization of social development programs (Wanak 2008, 206).

Psychological development provides the correct understanding of their identity as image bearers of God, the correct view of their God-given abilities, and the correct view of God's resources. Social development provides the correct understanding that they are loved and accepted by God and others, helps them understand that they are a part of God's family, and that they need people around them to journey together in life.

William Carey, "the father of modern missions", has set an example on how evangelical Christians should respond to the needs of the people in a holistic manner. In addition to preaching and planting churches in India, Carey worked on reforming the system and empowering the people through his advocacy and writings. Speaking out against the caste system, protesting "sati" (a practice among Hindus in India that burns a widow to death on her husband's pyre), teaching agriculture, and building systems of higher education in India are the examples of his holistic response to the needs of the people in India. He integrated all of these activities with his evangelistic efforts in order to help in the holistic development of the people (Tizon 2008, 22).

POVERTY IS USUALLY DEFINED IN
ECONOMIC TERMS

People in the West usually define poverty in terms of hunger. That idea of looking at poverty in terms of lack of food comes from UN Food and Agriculture Organization, which announced in 2009 that more than a billion people are suffering from hunger. The correlation between poverty and hunger was institutionalized in the UN's first Millennium Development Goal (MDG), which is "to reduce poverty and hunger" (Banerjee and Duflo 2011, 19). It could have been the influence of that definition that all of the evangelical Christian leaders interviewed and the poor people who participated in focus group discussion defined poverty in material terms. On the other hand, regardless of definitions, physical deprivation and hunger issues are the most immediate needs people face. Thus, one does not need to know a definition of poverty in order to explain poverty in material needs. They gave examples of lack of food, shelter, clothing, education, and healthcare. It is also interesting that very few of them realize the reality of poverty mindset and the reality of powerlessness in their current situation.

Only one third of them mentioned psychological aspects

like laziness and discipline as their understanding of poverty. Some of them said that not having a relationship with God is also poverty in spiritual sense. A very few talked about broken families and having no friends as poverty, most of them did not see poverty in social terms. Social and relational aspects seem to be the neglected facets of poverty. People are virtually connected via the Internet but the lack of face-to-face interaction with another human being as well as the lack of peace and happiness point to social poverty. Since economic poverty is visible, it is not unusual that all the evangelical Christian leaders and poor people defined poverty in economic terms. However, what is worth noting is the fact that very few of them defined poverty in psychological and social terms. Though social and psychological poverty is invisible it affects the poor even more than economic poverty. Evangelical Christians seem to think that psychological and social poverty is the result of spiritual poverty. Therefore, they define poverty in economic terms, and refer to spiritual poverty as the root of all poverty.

WIDESPREAD CORRUPTION

All of the evangelical Christian leaders and some of the poor people think that a corrupt and unjust political system is the primary reason behind the persistent problem of poverty in the Philippines. Almost all of them mentioned corruption in the government as one of the main reasons why there is so much poverty. According to the Social Weather Stations 2008 Survey of Enterprises on Corruption, three key government agencies are the most corrupt in the Philippines: the Bureau of Internal Revenue, the Bureau of Customs, and the Department of Public Works and Highways. Sixty percent of those participated in the SWS survey reported seeing "a lot of corruption" in the government sector. (SWS surveys business people to understand their perception of corruption in the country). ADB shows how poor people are impacted both directly and indirectly as a result of such widespread corruption in the government:

> "The impact of corruption on the poor can be determined through its direct impact (increased costs of social services, reduced quality of social

services, poor infrastructure, and restricted access to basic services such as water, electricity, health, and education and indirect impact (by redirecting public finances away from social sectors and constraining economic growth and poverty reduction)" (ADB 2009, 1579).

It reveals the sad reality of a well-established culture of corruption in all levels of the government. Dambisa Moyo in her book, *Dead Aid: Why Aid is not Working and How There is Another Way for Africa*, writes, "In a context of high degrees of corruption and uncertainty, fewer entrepreneurs (domestic or foreign) will risk their money in business ventures where corrupt officials can lay claim to its proceeds, so investment stagnates, and falling investment kills off growth" (Moyo 2009, 43). Moyo's assessment is true in the context of the Philippines, as systemic corruption in the government continues to hinder growth and keeps poverty persistent.

More than half of the focus group discussion participants alluded to the idea of vices in terms of persistence of poverty. They mentioned bad friends, drugs, alcohol, and gambling as reasons behind poverty that relate to social poverty. They also mentioned laziness, not having knowledge, no discipline, no respect, no hope, no confidence, no education, and being shy. Their response was mainly focused on the individual's choice and reasons that they can do something about. The research shows that the poor people see themselves as the reason behind poverty. They did not blame the government or rich people for this situation. Their response shows that they take responsibility for their poverty and the poverty of their community.

According to the World Risk Report 2014, "More than

half of the population of the Philippines live in disaster prone areas, and the country has the second greatest risk of disaster worldwide." However, it was interesting that the majority of the poor people did not mention the reality of natural disasters as one of the primary reasons for persistent poverty. It could be because they are based in Metro Manila where the effect of those natural disasters is not as disastrous as in some of the provinces. Because the country faces at least one or more natural calamities every year, it is likely one of the primary reasons for the persistence of poverty in the Philippines. According to ADB, "The proportion of households living below poverty line has declined very slowly and unevenly in the past four decades. Poverty alleviation has been much slower in the Philippines than in neighboring countries" (ADB 2009, 1). Thus, recurring natural disasters continue to push the country below poverty line comparing to other Southeast nations. I assume that the most of the poor people did not mention natural disasters because they are not able to see beyond the immediate situation that they are in.

However, it is interesting that population growth was not mentioned by either the evangelical Christian leaders or the poor people themselves as one of the causes of poverty. More than half of the poor people mentioned laziness, lack of discipline, and vices as the primary causes that keep poverty persistent. It is apparent that poor people in many ways see themselves as the primary reason why they are poor. Their response points to the reality of psychological poverty that is prevalent among the poor people which requires intentional psychological development.

LACK OF EDUCATION AND FINANCIAL LITERACY

Education seems to be one of the major factors in the persistence of poverty in the Philippines. Less than ten percent of the poor people interviewed went to college. Almost all the poor people who participated in focus group discussion only had elementary to high school level education. Thus, lack of educational attainment is one of the major reasons why they are in poverty. "Poverty levels are strongly linked to educational attainment. Two-thirds of poor households are headed by people with only an elementary school education or below. Access to quality education is identified as a key pathway out of poverty" (ADB 2009, 3). Education helps poor people to find a good-paying job, start a small business, or go into various professional careers. Thus, parents should make it a priority to provide best education to their children in order to get out of the cycle of poverty (Liuson 2015, 108).

> Education in all different forms is key to breaking the cycle of poverty. The relationship between poverty and education is complex, but we know that

education helps people make healthier and smarter decisions about their children, their livelihoods and the way they live (ChildFund 2018).

In addition, lack of financial literacy adds more to the persistence of poverty in the Philippines. According to the Vice President of the Philippines, Leni Robredo, "Poverty is a multi-faceted problem. There are times when a person stays poor despite working very hard to improve his situation . . . a good financial education provides them a fighting chance in pulling themselves up from poverty" (ABS-CBN News 2018).

ECONOMIC AND SPIRITUAL DEVELOPMENT USUALLY EMPHASIZED

My interviews with evangelical Christian leaders have consistently revealed their emphasis on economic and spiritual aspects of development. It could be evident even from their definition of poverty. This may suggest evangelical Christians typically believe that poverty is a lack of material things and a lack of relationship with God. That is why their response is focused on those areas of lack. Economic development helps meet the immediate needs of the poor and spiritual development helps meet the eternal need. In other words, saving lives on the earth by giving material needs and saving souls for heaven by proclaiming the Gospel. Almost every evangelical church, NGO, and INGO is integrating both economic and spiritual development in all of their programs and services. One of the reasons why they emphasize economic poverty is because it is evident everywhere. People are begging on the street, children are malnourished, families are sleeping under bridges and so on. It compels evangelical Christians to do something out of their compassionate heart for poor people. While responding to the needs of the poor, they usually share the Gospel for their eternal life as well.

A researcher on *Randomizing Religion: The Impact of Protestant Evangelism on Economic Outcomes* shows the impact of spiritual programs offered by evangelical Christians in the Philippines:

> To test the causal impact of religiosity, we conducted a randomized evaluation of an evangelical Protestant Christian values and theology education program that consisted of 15 weekly half-hour sessions. We analyze [sic] outcomes for 6,276 ultra-poor Filipino households six months after the program ended. We find [sic] significant increases in religiosity and income, no significant changes in total labor supply, assets, consumption, food security, or life satisfaction, and a significant decrease in perceived relative economic status (Bryan, Choi, and Karlan 2018, 1).

It is apparent that economic and spiritual development are the measuring sticks for many churches, NGOs, and INGOs in terms of their success. If poor people were provided with the necessary daily needs and an opportunity to hear the Gospel, then that would be a successful poverty response. It is evident that this emphasis on economic and spiritual development has served both physical and spiritual needs of the poor. It seems to be working well when intertwined with each other rather than separating one from the other. Economic and spiritual development is definitely the top priorities for evangelical Christians in their response to poverty.

PSYCHOLOGICAL AND SOCIAL DEVELOPMENT OFTEN OVERLOOKED

Based on my interviews with evangelical Christian leaders it seems that psychological and social development of the poor is not the main priorities of their programs and services. They do have programs and services to meet psychological and social needs of the poor, but they do not seem to be intentionally designed for psychological and social development. Maggie Black writes:

> Although the economic players have occupied development's commanding heights, those engaged in social progress have belatedly gained some recognition. That's the least they deserve. Most of the current wisdom comes from the social sphere, not the economic. Despite greater acknowledgement that development should focus on people's wellbeing, and not on national balance sheets, progress measured in terms of the human condition is still unsatisfactory (Black 2007, 1152).

One of the reasons for this is that psychological and

social poverty is not evident on the surface level as is economic and spiritual poverty. Another reason is that evangelical Christians are not equipped well to effectively respond to social and psychological needs. Thus, there is a need for evangelical Christians to understand the roots of social and psychological poverty.

Though psychological and social development is not the intentional priority of evangelical Christian response to poverty, psychological and social development of the poor is often expected. However, the poor people are concerned about their psychological well-being. Bryant Myers refers to the report of the Voices of the Poor project conducted by the World Bank in the early 2000s to listen to the world's poorest people. He argues that based on the voices of over sixty thousand poor people psychological well-being is their top most concern. Their desire to feel better, have a sense of dignity, wish for respect, have peace of mind, lack of anxiety, be God-fearing, and happy are some of the signs that poor people are in need of psychological development (Myers 2011, 1113).

In terms of evangelical Christian response to poverty in the Philippines, programs and services intended for economic development are also making psychological impact in the lives of the poor. When programs and services help in their economic situation, it gives them confidence and hope. The poor people seem to be empowered by the opportunities and exposure provided by evangelical programs and services for their economic development. On the other hand, programs and services intended for spiritual development are also making social impact in the lives of the poor. Most of the spiritual activities take place in a group setting where the beneficiaries are either required or encouraged to attend. It provides an opportunity for the poor people to find new friends, build relationships, form networks, and have a place to belong. It shows the fact that poor people are in need of intentional psychological and social development in addition to economic and spiritual development.

BAND-AID SOLUTION CREATES DEPENDENCY

Many of the evangelical Christian leaders I interviewed mentioned that a band-aid solution to poverty is one of the reasons why poverty has been persistent in the Philippines over the years. One of them said, "We do not fight poverty in a systematic way." The root of poverty is not addressed. Spiritual poverty is not addressed as part of poverty alleviation. Most of the efforts are dealing with the symptoms, not going deep into the root. Evangelical Christians have been giving much aid to the poor that is helpful for their immediate needs, but it will not solve the problem of poverty. William Easterly reminds the evangelical Christians in his book, *The White Man's Burden: Why the West's Effort to Aid the Rest Have Done So Much Ill and So Little Good,* saying, "Remember, aid cannot achieve the end of poverty. Only homegrown development based on the dynamism of individuals and firms in free markets can do that. Shorn of the impossible task of general economic development, aid can achieve much more than it is achieving now to relieve the sufferings of the poor" (Easterly 2006, 368). Only one third of the evangelical Christian leaders interviewed think that giving aid for a long period of time hinders the empowerment of the poor, which will result in the persistence of poverty. Giving aid to quick fix the problem of poverty has created an aid-dependent culture among the poor in the Philippines. Regarding quick-fix, Robert D. Lupton writes, "Top-down charity seldom works. Governments can give millions, rock bands can do benefit concerts, ex-presidents can champion causes, and churches can mobilize their volunteers. But in the end what takes place in the community, on the street, in the home, is what will ultimately determine the sustainability of any development" (Lupton 2011, 85).

The problem of sustainability became apparent when one of the leaders said, "There is no sustained effort in poverty alleviation." It is observed that the majority of the evangelical Christian response to poverty is still focused on providing the immediate need. It is like giving out fish always instead of teaching them how to fish on their own. Craig L. Bloomberg, distinguished professor of New Testament at Denver Seminary, puts it this way:

> It's not enough to throw at a need if it creates a sense of dependency and "enabling" (in the counseling sense of the term) that encourages people to continue to rely on outside support when they could be meeting their own needs. Christian leaders among even some of the poorest communities around the world acknowledge that church or community members could largely support indigenous work with some sacrifice, but see no reason to do so, as long as even larger amounts of money keep pouring in from the outside (Bloomberg 2013, 379).

Based on the interviews with evangelical Christian leaders, most of their response to poverty includes providing for immediate needs of the poor. It is necessary to provide for immediate needs when the poor people are in desperate need of food, clothes and shelter; but there must be an intentional plan to help in a sustainable manner. Evangelical Christians seem to provide for immediate needs as an entry point to begin their poverty alleviation efforts in a community. However, in many cases, they have been continually providing for immediate needs for several years. It shows the need for an integrated response to help in the economic, psychological, social, and spiritual development of the poor so they can be empowered to think about their development instead of being dependent.

LACK OF COLLABORATION IN
RESPONDING TO POVERTY

Interviews with evangelical Christian leaders led me to this conclusion that there is a lack of collaboration among evangelical Christians, government, and other national and international agencies that are responding to poverty in the Philippines. One of the evangelical Christian leaders I interviewed said, "Response to poverty is not well coordinated among various agencies." It seems that every church, NGO, and INGO is doing their own thing. There is also not much collaboration with the government and other humanitarian agencies. In many cases, lack of collaboration has created repetition of work which points to the fact that there may be subconscious competition among each other. There seems to be lot of resources and manpower that is not maximized well.

Several evangelical Christian leaders mentioned the need for better collaboration among evangelical Christians in responding to poverty. Instead of many churches doing small projects, they should join hands to help a poor community in a significant way. One of them also pointed out the need for an umbrella body of evangelical churches,

NGOs, and INGOs in responding to poverty. They all seem to echo the lack of evangelical Christian individuals', churches', NGOs', and INGOs' efforts to come together to create a poverty response plan and implement it by using their unique skills, manpower, and resources.

It is evident that there has been an unintended sense of competition among each other. Proper collaboration among evangelical Christians is crucial for a holistic response to poverty and for the holistic development of the poor. However, there seems to be no consensus in terms of a particular approach among evangelical Christians. It shows the reality of each individual church, NGO, and INGO doing their own thing without joining hands with others in responding to poverty. Their programs and services are working well in helping the poor, but a proper collaboration would definitely add strength to those individual efforts. I wholeheartedly believe that collaborated evangelical Christian response to poverty is crucial for poverty alleviation in the Philippines.

8

HOW SHOULD WE THEN RESPOND TO POVERTY?

When the economic, psychological, social, and spiritual poverty is addressed in an integrated manner, poor people will experience shalom which is the goal of holistic development. Since all of the evangelical Christian leaders interviewed and some of the poor people themselves refer to corrupt and unjust political system as one of the key reasons behind persistent poverty, the response must deal with those systems that keep the Filipino people poor. If not, "unfair systems cause and perpetuate the vicious cycle of poverty" (Keller Jr. 2012, 2522). Thus, evangelical Christian response to poverty should deal with the roots of a corrupt and unjust political system. One of ways to do so is to establish partnership with government agencies in various levels that could provide an opportunity for evangelical Christians to help transform the corrupt and unjust political system.

Likewise, since many evangelical Christian leaders mentioned recurring natural disasters are one of the causes of persistent poverty, the response must focus on disaster risk reduction awareness prior to calamity and rehabilitation of the poor after calamity. It helps in the empowerment and the sustainable development of the poor. Thus, there is a need for an intentional response to the root causes of poverty in addition to responding to its visible symptoms. Evangelical Christian response to poverty should be intentional in all four areas of development: physical, psychological, social, and spiritual in order to achieve the goal of holistic development of the poor. These are recommendations that may be of help to the evangelical Christians in responding to poverty. These recommendations are based on the findings of my research and they are intended to encourage the evangelical Christian churches, NGOs, and INGOs to respond to poverty economically, psychologically, socially, and spiritually.

EMPOWERING THE POOR

Since poverty is usually rooted in the mindset of the poor, there has to be a psychological response to poverty. However, only half of the evangelical churches, NGOs, and INGOs interviewed are intentionally responding to the psychological needs of the poor. In a statement, the Social Weather Stations (SWS) said 47 percent of the national population of the Philippines consider themselves poor according to an existing standard as of September 2017. The survey asked: Where would you place your family in this card? (Not poor, On the line, Poor). SWS conducted this survey using face-to-face interviews of 1,500 adults aged 18 years and above from Sept. 23 to 27.

The self-rating approach to poverty (SRP) measurement was designed in 1974 in the Social Indicators Project (SIP), which Mangahas directed at the Development Academy of the Philippines. In the SRP system, poverty is defined as whatever the people themselves associate with the word "mahirap." When first used at the national level in

April 1983, SRP was 55 percent. In the March 2002
Social Weather Survey, 58% of households in the
Philippines consider themselves mahirap or poor
(Reyes 2002, 50).

There seems to be an underlying assumption among
evangelical Christians that the economic and spiritual
response to poverty will result in psychological development of the poor. Thus, the focus has typically been on
meeting the physical needs of the poor and sharing the
Gospel. It has also been evident in this research that most of
the evangelical Christian churches, NGOs, and INGOs interviewed are giving aid as their response to the problem of
poverty in the Philippines. Aid is something that is given
when there is an immediate need. It is necessary in the
Philippines since there are natural disasters almost every
year. However, aid is not supposed to be a long-term
response to poverty because it creates dependency on the
side of the poor. Instead of giving aid to the poor year after
year, evangelical Christians should think of helping them
become self-sustainable over the years.

In terms of the process of empowering the poor, God's
empowerment to Gideon in the Bible to be an agent of
transformation serves as an example. Empowerment begins
with articulating the needs of the poor along with affirma-
tions of strength and opportunities. One of the first steps is
to help people identify their problems. Thus, there should
not be pre-packaged analyses; instead, evangelical Christians should facilitate people's participation in analyzing
their own situation (Wanak 2008, 60-61). Many churches,
NGOs, and INGOs have been feeding the poor, running
orphanages, and distributing relief goods for many years.
Evangelical Christian churches, NGOs, and INGOs need to

focus on empowering the poor to fish for themselves instead of giving fish for a prolonged period of time.

Steve Corbett and Brian Fikkert give an important reminder to the evangelical Christians in terms of empowering the poor, which is to avoid paternalism. They say, "Do not do things for people that they can do for themselves" (Corbett and Fikkert 2012, 109). A lot of times poor people need more than material things; they need new ideas and moral support. However, there is a huge difference between coming alongside the poor and doing things for them. Evangelical Christians should be intentional in helping the poor people to figure out their own plan for getting from where they are to where they want to be. This is not easy, it requires humility and generosity, but it is important to empower them (Gordon and Perkins 2013, 158). Psychological development is an essential aspect of the holistic development of the poor. So, I recommend evangelical Christians to have an intentional response to the psychological development of the poor in order to empower them.

PARTNERING WITH GOVERNMENT

In recent years, the relationship between "the country and the people" has been turning into the relationship between "the country and the person." People are beginning to have direct and individualized contact with the governments. The programs and services of the government to the people – from public school to energy subsidy – are turning into cash to be delivered via cell phone or debit card (Giugale 2014, 2). However, in the context of the Philippines, "poor people are often at the mercy of systems created by the powerful. Hence, poverty-alleviation efforts need to address both broken systems and broken individuals, using highly relational approaches wherever possible" (Corbett and Fikkert 2015, 171). Political dynasties that are dominant in the local government positions are usually associated with corruption (ADB 2009, 96). Thus, there is a great need for evangelical Christians to partner with the government in both national and local levels to help transform those corrupt and broken systems.

Evangelical Christians have a very minimal partnership with the government in terms of their poverty alleviation efforts. It is presumed that evangelical Christians usually go directly to the poor to avoid a long government process and not to let the government officials pocket the money that should go to the poor. As the ADB report says, "They are also directly involved in poverty alleviation in various ways, including soup kitchens, rice distribution, medical and funeral assistance, livelihood programs, and microfinance" (ADB 2009, 77). Those are valid reasons for direct involvement; but there is a need for transformation in the government system and evangelical Christians can play a vital role in that transformation. In his keynote address in the 2007 Lausanne Philippine Congress, David Lim challenged evangelical Christians to transform their churches into "center(s) for community transformation." He then added that the center should contribute to the national transformation and thereby show to the world the loving character of God. Since evangelical Christian churches, NGOs and INGOs interviewed work very closely with the poor, there is a need for them to partner with the government agencies. Such partnership helps in complementing the programs and services of the government.

Government plays a very important role in alleviating poverty. According to ADB, "the state's response to poverty is crucial in terms of how deeply and quickly poverty can be reduced" (ADB 2009, 96). There is no other way to alleviate poverty in the Philippines if the government sector continues its practices in terms of corruption, unjust political systems and weak local government. However, the evangelical Christians should realize that the government is still the legitimate body responsible for poverty alleviation. Likewise, the government should recognize the importance of the involvement of evangelical Christian churches, NGOs, and INGOs in meeting the needs of the poor (Olarinmoye

2012, 11). One of the ways for the government to do so it by looking at the growth rate of evangelical Christians in the country. Government can also take note of the key evangelical Christian INGOs that are responding to poverty. Evangelical Christians' partnership with government agencies on the local level is even more important so their expertise, resources and manpower can supplement the resources and manpower of the government agencies. The researcher recommends that evangelical Christian churches, NGOs, and INGOs work in partnership with various branches of the government. So that government officials will be able to witness Christian love in words and in actions. As a result, government officials and the various branches of the government they serve will experience transformation.

One of the examples of partnering in government transformation is the "Memoranda of Agreement" between International Graduate School of Leadership (IGSL) and different branches of the military and law enforcement of the Philippines. IGSL is one of the PCNC accredited evangelical Christian NGOs that is committed to train government officials in "Transformational Leadership." One of the graduates of IGSL, Lieutenant Colonel John Jadloc says:

> IGSL teaches leadership by demonstrating it. Each faculty member leads a group of students and journeys with them throughout the course. The MATL program helped me understand the prevailing culture of the Armed Forces of the Philippines. It equipped me to be an effective advocate of good governance through the Army Transformation Roadmap. IGSL provided knowledge and skills that helped me contribute to personal and organizational transformation by, for

instance, helping people resolve personal conflicts. All of these are in light of continuous study, teaching and practice of the Word of God (IGSL 2018).

After graduating from IGSL, John served with the Army Governance System Management Office, the office driving the implementation of the Army Transformation Roadmap. IGSL envisions a growing network of Christ-like leaders building spiritual movements, exerting moral influence, and transforming nations for the glory of God (IGSL 2018).

COLLABORATING WITH OTHERS

Samuel Jayakumar, one of the contributors in the book, *The Church and Poverty in Asia*, writes about the need for evangelical Christians to come together as brothers and sisters to respond to needs of the poor. Throughout the Bible, God reveals his concern and compassion for the poor. It is a clear indication of what Christians should be doing for them. The local church should be seen as the largest NGO or INGO in the world. Likewise, NGOs and INGOs should be viewed as a part of that church to carry out its mission. Thus, the collective body of Christ has a great responsibility to respond to the needs of the poor (Wanak 2008, 74). I see the need to form an umbrella organization which includes evangelical Christian churches, NGOs, and INGOs that are working with the poor. It would function as a unified body to bring all evangelicals together for a more coordinated and collaborated response to poverty in the Philippines. The proposed umbrella organization would help bring those individual efforts together to provide a bigger picture of the evangelical Christian response to poverty. It would provide strength as churches, NGOs, and INGOs become more aware of each other's work, resources, and manpower. It would serve like a multi-stringed rope in terms of evangelical Christian response to poverty to help in the economic, psychological, social, and spiritual development of the poor.

One third of the evangelical Christian leaders mentioned during the interview that there is a need for collaboration among Christians in responding to poverty. Local churches are concerned that many NGOs and INGOs are not partnering with a local church when they do their projects and provide services. Bryant Myers, professor of transformational development at Fuller Theological Seminary, puts it this way:

> The church represents a special challenge to many involved in Christian development, since much of the work in the last quarter-century has been done by the so-called para-church agencies. Made up of Christians, these agencies go directly to Christians in the pews to solicit funds and then directly to poor communities to help the poor. The local church on both ends is too frequently ignored, or worse, seen as part of the problem. This is a seriously flawed view (Myers 2011, 2064).

In some cases, NGOs and INGOs themselves are competing with each other to respond to the poor rather than collaborating each other. While in other instances, local churches are also responding to poverty on their own without joining hands with NGOs and INGOs.

There is a need for evangelical Christians in the Philippines to consider Acts 2:42-47 in their response to poverty. The first disciples lived out their Christian life and stood together against poverty. The Holy Spirit empowered them to create their new identity and belonging in God's family. There was a great deal of collaboration in the body of Christ and God blessed them (Barker 2009, 2178). The same kind of collaboration among the evangelical Christians is necessary for effective response to poverty. With proper collaboration, beneficiaries of NGOs and INGOs can be easily channeled to a local church in terms of their continual spiritual growth and fellowship. Likewise, beneficiaries and members of the local churches will be able to volunteer in NGOs and INGO efforts in their community. Coordination consumes both time and resources, but it is necessary in order to be able to craft well-designed and efficiently implemented programs" (ADB 2009, 67). Therefore, the I would recommend a better coordination among evangelical Christian churches, NGOs, and INGOs in order to have a better collaboration in responding to poverty.

RESPONDING IN HOLISTIC MANNER

Timothy Keller, pastor of Redeemer Church writes about the role of evangelical Christians in the holistic response to the needs of the poor, saying:

> Many believe that the job of the church is not to do justice at all, but the preach the Word, to evangelize and build up believers. But if it is true that justice and mercy to the poor are the inevitable signs of justifying faith, it is hard to believe that the church is not to reflect this duty corporately in some way. You can't love people in word only (cf. 1 John 3:16-17) and therefore you can't love people as you are doing evangelism and discipleship without meeting practical and material needs through deeds (Keller 2010, 135).

Evangelical Christian churches, NGOs, and INGOs should be intentionally involved in responding to the economic, psychological, social, and spiritual needs of the poor. Holistic development framework practitioners argue that these four kinds of poverty are connected with each other. Thus, to deal with all four kinds of poverty, there is a need for an integrated response that includes economic, psychological, social, and spiritual development of the poor. However, majority of the evangelical Christian churches, NGOs, and INGOs are involved in addressing the economic and spiritual needs of the poor. These are two major areas of need that evangelical Christians should continue to address. In addition, evangelical Christians should consider psychological and social needs being as important as the physical and spiritual needs. During the 1990s the World Bank asked the basic question, "What is poverty?" to more than sixty thousand poor from sixty poor countries. The results of this study have been published in a three-volume book series called "Voices of the Poor." The poor people described their situation in psychological and social terms in addition to economic terms. They used the words like: shame, powerlessness, voicelessness, hopelessness, fear, inferiority, social isolation, and humiliation (Corbett and Fikkert 51).

It is easy to do a feeding program once a week, give away used clothes once a month and organize a Christmas party once a year for the poor in their communities. But, to do intentional holistic ministry among the poor requires much intentionality, effort, and manpower. Preaching the gospel to the poor (Matthew 11:15, Luke 4:18) as Christ did is a very important aspect of responding to the spiritual needs of the poor. But, Jesus also fed the 4000 and the 5000 and did various ministries responding to the physical and spiritual needs of the people. He ate with sinners and tax collectors and He accepted them as they were. He taught his followers and helped them understand who He is and why He came. In other words, Jesus responded to the needs of people in a holistic manner. Amy L. Sherman shows how evangelical Christians should be holistic in their response to poverty:

> Imagine a large congregation with numerous professionals in the pews. Let's compare two possible strategies for serving its city. First, the church can partner with the local homeless shelter in providing the manpower to provide dinner once a month. Alternatively, it can encourage launching vocationally based small groups with the mandate to brainstorm how they can deploy their particular vocational skills and networks to help address poverty locally. In the first instance, the church treats its bankers, doctors, accountants, lawyers, and business owners generically — as bodies that can ladle soup. In the latter approach, the church challenges these same congregants to think creatively about how to use the unique gifts God has given them to bring a greater taste of shalom to the community (Sherman 2018).

Though poverty is typically defined as a condition of people with lowness of income (Sen 1999, 87), "the problem of poverty goes well beyond material dimension, so the solutions must go beyond the material as well" (Corbett and Fikkert 2013, 51). Integrated response to economic, psychological, social, and spiritual poverty would result in holistic development of the poor.

CONCLUDING REMARKS

Evangelical Christians are still a very small group compared to the majority Roman Catholic population in the Philippines which has also been responding to poverty over the years. Therefore, evangelical Christians should neither solely take credit for poverty alleviation nor take blame for the persistence of poverty in the Philippines. Instead, they should continue to respond to poverty by focusing on holistic development of the poor.

REFERENCE LIST

Ababa, Rizalina L. 2011. "Transforming Lives and Communities: A case study on
   building partnerships in the Philippines through Appreciative Inquiry." SIT Graduate Institute.

ABS-CBN. Last Modified on April 28, 2017. Accessed on May 3, 2018.
   http://news.abs-cbn.com/news/04/28/17/50-percent-of-pinoys-say-they-are-poor-sws

ABS-CBN News. "Financial literacy key to helping poor rise from poverty, Robredo
   says." Last Modified on May 6, 2018. Accessed on May 12, 2018.   http://news.abs-cbn.com/news/05/06/18/financial-literacy-key-to-helping-poor-rise-from-poverty-robredo-says

Adamo, David. 2001. "Peace in the Old Testament and African Heritage" *Explorations*
   Pages 109-26 in African Studies. Eugene, OR: Wipf and Stock Publishers.

Asian Development Bank. 2018. *Poverty in the Philippines.* "Poverty Data Philippines."

Accessed on April 27, 2018. https://www.adb.org/countries/philippines/poverty

Ahorro, Joseph. 2008. "The Waves of Post-Development Theory and a Consideration of

the Philippines." University of Alberta.

Aldaba, Fernando. 2009. *Poverty in the Philippines: Causes, Constraints and*

Opportunities. Mandaluyong City: Asian Development Bank.

Allen, Tim and Alan Thomas. eds. 2000. *Poverty and Development: Into the 21st*

Century. 2nd ed. New York: Oxford University Press.

Archer, Colin. 1980. *Poverty – The Church's Abandoned Revolution: A Scientific,*

Biblical and Theological Commentary. Nassau, Bahamas: Colmar Publications, Inc.

Armstrong, Aaron. 2011. *Awaiting a Savior: The Gospel, the New Creation, and the End*

of Poverty. Ohio: Cruciform Press.

ATD Fourth World. "Measuring Poverty." Accessed on April 5, 2017.

http://www.atdfourthworld.org/internationaladvocacy/measuring-poverty/

Baker, Ash. 2009. *Make Poverty Personal: Taking the Poor as Seriously as the Bible*
Does. Grand Rapids, MI: Baker Books.

Baker, David L. 2009. *Tight Fists or Open Hands: Wealth and Poverty in Old Testament*
Law. Grand Rapids, Michigan: Eerdmans.

Banerjee, Abhijit V. and Esther Duflo. 2011. *Poor Economics: A Radical Rethinking of*
the Way to Fight Global Poverty. New York, NY: Public-Affairs.

Barber, Leroy. 2016. *Embrace: God's Radical Shalom for a Divided World*. Downers
Grove, IL: Intervarsity Press.
Beed, Clive and Cara Beed. 2006. *Alternatives to Economics: Christian Socio-economic*
Perspectives. Lanham, MD: University Press of America.

Berkman, Elliot. 2015. "Its not a lack of self control that keeps people poor." The
Conversation. Last Modified September 22, 2015. Accessed January 16, 2018. http://theconversation.com/its-not-a-lack-of-self-control-that-keeps-people-poor-47734

Bersales, Lisa Grace S. Philippine Statistics Authority. "Farmers, Fishermen and
Children consistently posted the highest poverty incidence among basic sectors." Last Modified June 30, 2017. Accessed July 28, 2017. https://psa.gov.ph/poverty-press-releases

Birch, Bruce C. and Larry Rasmussen. *A Difficult Text: For You Always Have the Poor*
    with You. Boston College, C21 Resources. The Church in the 21st Century Center. Fall 2014.

Bjoraker, William D. 2012. "The Restoration of Shalom." William Carey International
    Development Journal. Last Modified September 24. Accessed April 12, 2017. http://www.wciujournal.org/blog/post/the-restoration-of-shalom

Black, Maggie, 2007. *The No-Nonsense Guide to International Development.* Oxford,
    UK: New Internationalist Publications Ltd.

Bloomberg, Craig L. 1999. *Neither Poverty nor Riches: A Biblical Theology of*
    Possessions. Downers Grove, IL: Intervarsity Press.

_____. 2013. *Christians in an Age of Wealth: A Biblical Theology of*
    Stewardship. Grand Rapids, MI: Zondervan.

Boas, Taylor C. & Jordan Gans-Morse. 2009. "Neoliberalism: From New Liberal
    Philosophy to Anti-Liberal Slogan." Volume 44, Issue 2 (June): 137–161.

Boundless. "Measuring Poverty." Accessed April 8, 2017.
    https://www.boundless.com/sociology/textbooks/boundless-sociology-textbook/stratification-inequality-and-social-class-in-the-u-s-9/poverty-78/measuring-poverty-463-3312/

Bosch-Heij, Deborah van den. 2012. *Spirit and Healing in Africa: A Reformed Pneumatological Perspective*. Westdene, Bloemfontein: Rapid Access Publishers.

Bradley, Anne and Art Lindsley, eds. 2014. *For the Least of These: A Biblical Answer to Poverty*. Bloomington, IN: WestBow.

Bradshaw, Ted K. 2006. *"Theories of Poverty and Anti-Poverty Programs in Community Development." Rural Poverty Research Center*: Working Paper No. 06-05.

Bryan, Gharad T., James J. Choi, and Dean Karlan. 2018. "Randomizing Religion: The Impact of Protestant Evangelism on Economic Outcomes." NBER Working Paper No. 24278.

Callanta, Ruth S. "A Transformational Strategy: Toward Filling the Hungry with Good Things." In Book, edited by Lee Wanak, 147-162. 1st Edition ed. Mandaluyong: OMF Literature, 2008.

Cheong, John and Eloise Meneses. Eds. 2015. *Christian Mission and Economic Systems: A Critical Survey of the Cultural and Religious Dimensions of Economies*. Pasadena, CA: William Carey Library.

Chester, Tim. 2013. *Good News to the Poor: Sharing the Gospel through Social Involvement*. Wheaton, IL: Crossway.

ChildFund. 2018. "Poverty and Education." Accessed May 13, 2018.
   https://www.childfund.org/about-us/education/

Chojnicki, Zbyszko. 2010. "Socio-Economic Development and Its Axiological Aspects."
   Institute of Socio-Economic Geography and Spatial Management. Adam Mickiewicz University, Poznań, Poland.

Christian, Jaykumar. 2011. *God of the Empty-Handed: Poverty, Power and the Kingdom*
   of God. Victoria, Australia: Acron Press Ltd.

CIA World Factbook. 2015. "Population below poverty line: Philippines." Last Modified
   June 30. Accessed March 7, 2018. https://www.indexmundi.com/g/g.aspx?c=rp&v=69

Clifford, Paula. April 2010. *Theology and International Development. A Christian Aid*
   Report. Christian Aid.

Cloud-Townsend Resources. 2001. "Spiritual Poverty." How People Grow. Last
   Modified July 28. Accessed March 16, 2017. http://www.cloudtownsend.com/spiritual-poverty/

Costas, Orlando. 1986. "Evangelical Theology in the Two Third World" in Mark Lau
   Branson and C. Rene Padilla (eds.). *Conflict and Context: Hermeneutics in the Americas*. Grand Rapids, MI: Eerdmans.

Cowen, M.P., and R.W. Shenton. 1996. *Doctrines of Develop-*

ment. New York:
    Routledge. Dang, Giang and Sui Pheng Low. 2015. *Infrastructure Investments in Developing Economies: The Case of Vietnam.* Singapore: Springer.

Curtis, Heather D. 2018. *Holy Humanitarians: American Evangelicals and Global Aid.*
    Cambridge, MA: Harvard University Press.

Danker, Frederick William, eds. 2000. *A Greek-English Lexicon of the New Testament*
    and Other Early Christian Literatures. Third Edition (BDAG). Chicago: University of Chicago Press.

David Kotter. Accessed on December 18, 2016.
    https://tifwe.org/sin-the-root-cause-of- poverty/

Dean, Judith M. and Julie Schaffner. eds. 2005. *Attacking Poverty in the Developing*
    World: Christian Practitioners and Academics in Collaboration. California: Authentic & World Vision.

Development Asia. Expanding the Philippines' Pantawid Program. POLICY BRIEF. May
    2016. Accessed on October 4, 2016. http://development. asia/policy-brief/expanding-philippines-pantawid-program

DomNwachukwu, Chinaka S. and Heekap Lee. 2014. *Multiculturalism: A Shalom Motif*
    for the Christian Community. Eugene, OR: Wipf and Stock Publishers.

Drake, Martin. 2013. "Do You Know the Definition of Poverty." The Borgen Project.

   Last Modified July 29. Accessed March 7, 2017. https://
borgenproject.org/do-you-know-the-definition-of-poverty/

Easterly, William. 2006. *The White Man's Burden: Why the West's Effort to Aid the Rest*
   Have Done so Much Ill And So Little Good. New York: Penguin Books.

Economic and Social Inclusion Cooperation. 2008-2009. *What is Social Development?*
   New Nouveau Brunswick: Canada.

Economics Online. "Poverty." Accessed March 26, 2017.
   http://www.economicsonline.co.uk/
Managing_the_economy/Poverty.html

Elwell, Walter A. 1997. *"Entry for 'Poor and Poverty, Theology of'". "Evangelical*
   Dictionary of Theology". Grand Rapids, MI: Baker Book House Company.

Encyclopedia Britannica. 2011. "Poverty." Last Modified November 17. Accessed March
   28, 2017. https://www.britannica.com/topic/poverty

Eschooltoday. "Factors that cause poverty." Accessed April 22, 2017.
   http://www.eschooltoday.com/poverty-in-the-world/
causes-of-poverty.html

Escobar, Arturo. 1995. *Encountering Development: The Making and Unmaking of the*

Third World. Princeton, NJ: Princeton University Press.

Faith. 2013. "Shalom: A Beautiful Word of Many Meanings." Last Modified June 22.
Accessed April 9, 2017. https://israelmediaministries. jimdo.com/2013/06/22/shalom-a-beautiful-word-of-many-meanings/

Ferraro, Vincent. 2008. "Dependency Theory: An Introduction." *The Development*
Economics Reader. Ed. Giorgio Secondi (London: Routledge).

Fikkert, Brian and Steve Corbett. 2014. *When Helping Hurts: How to Alleviate Poverty*
Without Hurting the Poor...And Yourself. Chicago, IL: Moody Publishing.

Foote, Russell John. 2016. "Reconceptualizing Development: A Linkages-of-Capital
Approach." *Global Journal of Human-Social Science Research*. Last modified January 14. Accessed September 12, 2017. https://socialscienceresearch.org/index.php/GJHSS/article/view/1624

Fritz, Jan Marie. 2010. *Social and Economic Development: Socioeconomic*
Developmental Social Work. Vol. I. United Nations Education, Scientific and Cultural Organization. United Kingdom: Eolss Publishing Co. Ltd.

George, Timothy. 1999. "If I am an Evangelical, What Am I?" *Christianity Today*.

9 August.

Giugale, Marcelo M. 2014. *Economic Development: What Everyone Needs to Know.*
New York, NY: Oxford University Press.

Gordon, Wayne and John M. Perkins. 2013. *Making Neighborhoods Whole: A Handbook*
for Christian Community Development. Downers Grove, IL: InterVarsity Press.

Gorospe-Jamon, Grace and Mary Grace P. Mirandilla. "Religion and Politics: A look at
the Philippine Experience." In book, edited by Rodolfo C. Severino and Lprraine Carlos Salazar, Pages 100 – 127. 1st ed. Singapore: Institute of Southeast Asian Studies, 2007.

Greig, Alastair, David Hulme and Mark Turner. 2007. *Challenging Global Inequality:*
Development Theory and Practice in the 21st Century. New York: Palgrave Macmillan.

Groody, Daniel G. *The Option for the Poor in Christian Theology.* Notre Dame, Ind.:
University of Notre Dame Press, 2007.

Grudem, Wayne A. 2004. *Systematic Theology: An Introduction to Biblical Doctrine.*
Grand Rapids, MI: Zondervan Pub. House.

Grudem, Wayne and Barry Asmus. 2013. *The Poverty of Nations: A Sustainable Solution.*
Wheaton, IL: Crossway.

Guzman, Lawrence de. 2011. Philippine Daily Inquirer. "Philippines still top Christian
country in Asia, 5th in world." Last Modified December. Accessed August 6, 2017. http://globalnation.inquirer.net/ 21233/philippines-still-top-christian-country-in-asia-5th-in-world

Harriss, John. 2014. "Development Theories." Pp. 35-49 in *International*
Development: Ideas, Experience, and Prospects, edited by Bruce Currie-Alder, Ravi Kanbur, David M. Malone, and Rohinton Medhora. Oxford: Oxford University Press.

Harvey, David. 2005. *A Brief History of Neoliberalism.* Oxford: Oxford University Press.

Hayami, Yujiro and Yoshihisa Godo. 2005. *Development Economics: From the Poverty*
to the Wealth of Nations. 3rd ed. Oxford: Oxford University Press.

Heck, Stephanie. 2014. "Relieving Relational Poverty." *More Simply Human.* Last
Modified June 8. Accessed April 11, 2017. https:// moresimplyhuman.com/2014/06/08/relieving-relational-poverty/

Heifer the Philippines. Accessed on August 14, 2016.
https://www.heifer.org/ending-hunger/our-work/countries/asia/philippines.html

Hickman, Janet S. 2011. *Fast Facts for the Faith Community Nurse: Implementing*

FCN/Parish Nursing in a Nutshell. New York, NY: Springer Publishing Company.

Hoksbergen, Roland. 2012. *Serving God Globally: Finding Your Place in International*
    Development. Michigan: Baker Academic.

Holman, Susan R. 2008. *Wealth and Poverty in Early Church and Society.* Holy Cross
    Studies in Patristic Theology and History. Grand Rapids, MI: Brookline, Holy Cross Orthodox Press.

_____ 2009. *God Knows There's Need: Christian Responses to Poverty.*
    Oxford: Oxford University Press.

Hoppe, Leslie j. 2004. *There Shall Be No Poor among You: Poverty in The Bible.*
    Nashville: Abingdon Press.

Hove, Hilary. 2004. "Critiquing Sustainable Development: A Meaningful Way of
    Mediating the Development Impasse." *Undercurrent* Volume I, No 1.

Howitt, Quinton. 2012. *Christianity and the Poor.* Quinton Howitt Publications.

International Graduate School of Leadership. 2018. "MA in Transformational Leadership
    for the Uniformed Services." Accessed March 12, 2018. http://www.igsl.asia/matl-for-strategic-sectors-2/

Jaffee, David. 1998. *Levels of Socio-economic Development Theory.* 2nd ed. Westport, CT:
Praeger Publishers.

Jaykumar Christian. 1999. *God of the Empty-Handed.* MARC.
Joshua Project. 2017. Country: Philippines. Accessed July 15, 2017.
https://joshuaproject.net/countries/RP

Keller, Timothy. 2010. *Generous Justice: How God's Grace Makes Us Just.* Hudson
Street, NY: Penguin Group (USA) Inc.

Keller, Jack A. Jr. Ed. 2012. *Poverty.* New York, NY: United Methodist Women, Inc.

Kingsbury, Damien, Joe Remenyi, John McKay and Janet Hunt. 2004. *Key Issues in*
Development. New York: Palgrave Macmillan.

Kippler, Caroline. 2010. "Exploring Post-Development: Politics, the State and
Emancipation. The question of alternatives." *POLIS Journal* Vol. 3 (Winter).

Koehler, Ludwig, Walter Baumgartner, and M. E. J. Richardon. eds. 2000. *The Hebrew*
and Aramaic Lexicon of the Old Testament. Leiden: Brill Academic Publishers.

Lal, Deepak. 2002. *The Poverty of Development Economics.* London: The Institute of
Economic Affairs.

Landfair, Valerie. 2014. "Obgu Kalu, African Pentecostalism and Shalom." *CCDA pages*
    24-33 Theological Journal, 2014 Edition. Eds. Soong Chan Rah, Chanequa Walker-Barnes and Brandon Wrencher. CCDA Publishing.

Larrain, Jorge. 1989. *Theories of Development: Capitalism, Colonialism and*
    Dependency. Cambridge: Polity Press.

Leitner, Helga, Jamie Peck, and Eric Sheppard. eds. 2007. *Contesting Neoliberalism:*
    Urban Frontiers. New York: Guilford Press.

Levitas, R. A. 2006. "The concept and measurement of social exclusion." In C. Pantazis,
    D. Gordon, & R. Levitas (Eds.), *Poverty and social exclusion in Britain: the millennium survey* (pp. 123 - 160). Policy Press.

Liuson, Andrew. 2015. *The Debt-Free Lifestyle: Ten Principles that Can Revolutionize*
    Your Life. Makati, Philippines: Cross Over.

Longenecker, Bruce W. *Poverty and Paul's Gospel.* EX AUDITU, Vol. 27 / 2011.

Lupton, Robert. 2011. *Toxic Charity: How the Church Hurts Those They Help and How*
    to Reverse It. New York: HarperOne.

M Libraries. "The Consequences of Poverty." Social Problems: Continuity and Change.
    Accessed March 29, 2017. http://open.lib.umn.edu/

socialproblems/chapter/2-4-the-consequences-of-poverty/

Mani, Anandi, Sendhil Mullainathan, Eldar Shafir, and Jiaying Zhao. 2013. "Poverty
Impedes Cognitive Function." *Science*. Vol. 341, Issue 6149.

Makabenta, Yen. 2017. "Protestantism: The fastest growing religion in the developing
world." Last Modified November 18, 2017. Accessed February 20, 2018.
http://www.manilatimes.net/protestantism-fastest-growing-religion-developing-world/363522/

Martinussen, John. 1997. *Society, State and Market: A Guide to Competing Theories of
Development*. London: Zed Books.

Mitchell, Kenneth R. *Justice and Generosity: The Teaching of the Bible Concerning the
Poor*. Baltimore, Publish America Inc., 2008.

Moffett, Samuel H. 2005. *A History of Christianity in Asia. Volume II*. Maryknoll, NY:
Orbis Books.

Moffitt, Bob. 2006. *If Jesus Were Mayor: How God Can Use Your Church To Transform
Your Community*. Phoenix, AZ: Harvest Foundation.

_____. 2007. "Jesus' Model for Growth and Service." Phoenix, AZ: Disciple
Nations Alliance.

Moyo, Dambisa. 2009. Dead Aid: Why Aid Is Not Working and How There Is a Better
Way for Africa. New York, NY: Penguin Books.

Myers, Allen C. 1987. *The Eerdmans Bible Dictionary*. Grand Rapids, MI: Eerdmans.

Myers, Bryant. 1999. *Walking with the Poor: Principles and Practices of*
Transformational Development. Maryknoll, NY: Orbis Books.

Noel, Jean G. 2014. *How to Overcome the Spirit of Poverty*. CreateSpace Independent
Publishing Platform.

Nowers, Burt and Randy Steger. 2013. "Christian Relief and Development and Its Role
in Holistic Mission." *Leaven*: Vol. 21: Iss. 1, Article 3.

Olarinmoye, Omobolaji O. 2012. "Faith-Based Organizations and Development:
Prospects and Constraints." *Transformation: An International Journal of Holistic Mission Studies*. 29:1.

Olsen, Andrew. 2016. "Evangelicals and International Aid: Insights from a Landscape
Survey of U.S. Churches." Medford, MA: The Fletcher School, Tufts University.

Offutt, Stephen, F. David Bronkema, Robb Davis, Gregg Okesson, and Krisanne
Vaillancourt Murphy. 2016. *Advocating for Justice: An*

Evangelical Vision for Transforming Systems and Structures. Grand Rapids, MI: Baker Academic.

Parker, Canice. 2010-2012). "Mental Poverty and Factors of Poverty- Reasons for
   Famine." *Motivational Articles I.* Accessed March 29, 2017.
   http://www.positivepointofview.com/mental-poverty-reasons-for-famine.php

Peet, Richard and Elaine Hartwick. 2015. *Theories of Development: Contentions,*
   Arguments, Alternatives. 3rd ed. New York: Guliford Press.
   Perkins, John M. 1993. *Beyond Charity: The Call to Christian Community Development.*
   Baker Books.

Pew Research Center's Religion and Public Life Projects. 2010. "Global Religious
   Futures." Philippines. Religious Demography: Affiliation. Accessed July 27, 2017. http://www.globalreligiousfutures.org/countries/philippines#/?
   affiliations_religion_id=0&affiliations_year=2010&region_-name=All%20Countries&restrictions_year=2015

Philippine Council for NGO Certification. "The Role of Philippine NGOs." In
   Philippines Council for NGO Certification - Background and Rationale. Accessed August 7, 2017. http://www.pcnc.com.ph/pcnc-rationale.php

Philippine Council of Evangelical Churches. "PCEC Statements." Accessed July 24,
   2017. http://pceconline.org/prelease.htm

Philippine Daily Inquirer March 18, 2016.

Philippines Statistics Authority. 2016. "Highlights of the Philippine Population 2015
    Census of Population." Last Modified May 19. Accessed February 15, 2018.
        https://psa.gov.ph/content/highlights-philippine-population-2015-census-population

Pieterse, Jan Nederveen. 2000. "After Post-Development." *Third World Quarterly*. Vol.
    21, No. 2 (April): Taylor & Francis, Ltd.

Pixley, Jorge and clodovis Boff. 1989. *The Bible, the Church and the Poor: The Biblical,*
    Theological and Pastoral Aspects of the Option for the Poor. Tunbridge Wells, Great Britain: Burns and Oates Ltd.

Poverty Analysis (Summary), Accessed September 16, 2016.
        https://www.adb.org/sites/default/files/linked-documents/cps-phi-2011-2016-pa.pdf

Rachel Cannon. 2014. *"What are the Causes of Poverty?"* The Borgen Project. Last
    Modified June 22. Accessed March 17, 2017 https://borgenproject.org/causes-poverty/

Rapley, John. 2007. *Understanding Development: Theory and Practice in the Third*
    World. 3rd ed. Boulder, CO: Lynne Rienner Publisher.

Relational Thinking. "Relational Poverty." 2011. Accessed April 4, 2017.

http://relationalthinking.net/relational-poverty/

Rensburg, Janse van J., 2013. "The psychology of poverty."
Verbum et Ecclesia 34 (1)
    http://dx.doi.org/10.4102/ve.v34i1.825

Reyes, Celia M. 2002. "The Poverty Fight: Have We Made an
Impact?" *Philippines*
    Institute for Development Studies Discussion Paper. Series
No. 2002–20.

Reyes, Giovanni E. 2001. "Four Main Theories of Development: Modernization,
    Dependency, Word-System, and Globalization."
NOMADS.4.

Rhee, Helen. 2012. *Loving the Poor, Saving the Rich: Wealth,
Poverty, and Early*
    Christian Formation. Grand Rapids, MI: Baker
Academic.

Rist, Gilbert. 2008. *The History of Development: From Western
Origins to Global Faith*.
    3rd ed. London: Zed Books.

Rocamora, Joel, Hanneke van Eldik Thieme, and Ernesto M.
Hilario. eds. 1992.
    European official development assistance to the Philippines.
Manila: Transnational Institute and Council for People's
Development.

Ronsvalle, John and Sylvia Ronsvalle. 1992. *The Poor Have
Faces: Loving Your*

Neighbor in the 21ˢᵗ Century. Grand Rapids, MI: Baker Book House.

Roux Johan. 2007. *Empowering Destitute People towards Shalom: A Contextual*
   Missiological Study. University of South Africa.

Rowe, James E., ed. 2009. *Theories of Local Economic Development: Linking Theory*
   to Practice. England: Ashgate Publishing Limited.

Royal Geographical Society with IBG. 2013. "Theories of Development." Global
   Learning Programme. Accessed June 15, 2016. http://www.rgs.org/OurWork/Schools/Teaching+resources/Key+Stage+3+resources/Global+Learning+Programme/Theories+of+development.htm.

Sachs, Jeffrey D. 2015. *The End of Poverty*. Hudson Street, NY: Penguin Books.

Sané, Pierre. 2001. *The Role of the Social and Human Sciences in the Fight Against*
   Poverty. MOST-Newsletter, 10 UNESCO.

Save the Children Philippines. 2018. "Empowering Children Through Education."
   Accessed May 3, 2018. https://www.savethechildren.org.ph/our-work/the-challenges/education

Sen, Amartya. 1983. *"Poor, Relatively Speaking"* Oxford *Economic Papers*, New Series,
   Vol. 35 No. 2, July 1983.

_____. 1999. *Development as Freedom*. Oxford: Oxford University Press.

Severino, Rodolfo C. and Lorraine Carlos Salazar. 2007. *Whither the Philippines in the*
21st *Century?* Singapore: Institute of Southeast Asian Studies.

Shah, Shelly. 2013-2015. "Development: Essay on Human Development." Sociology
Discussion. Accessed June 14, 2016. http://www. sociologydiscussion.com/society/development-essay-on-human-development-2/1051.

Sheppard, Eric, Philip W. Porter, David R. Faust and Richa Nagar. 2009. *A World of*
Difference: Encountering and Contesting Development. 2nd ed. New York: Guliford Press.

Sherman, Amy L. 2018. "Hand Out or Hand Up?: Empowering the Poor." *Enrichment*
Journal. Springfield, MO: The General Council of Assemblies of God.

Siddiqui, Kalim. 2012. "Developing Countries' Experience with Neoliberalism
and Globalisation." *Research in Applied Economics*. Vol. 4, No. 4. Macrothink Institute.

Sider, Ronald J. 2005. *Rich Christians In An Age Of Hunger: Moving from Affluence to*
Generosity. Nashville, TN: Thomas Nelson.

Simkins, Ronald A. and Thomas M. Kelly. Eds. 2014. *The Bible, the Economy, and the*
  Poor. Journal of Religion & Society. Creighton University.

Sine, Christine. 2006. *GodSpace: Time for Peace in Rhythms of Life*. Newberg, OR:
  Barclay Press.

Smith, Adam.1776. *An Inquiry in to the Nature and Causes of the Wealth of Nations*.
  Edited by S. M. Soares. MetaLibri Digital Library, 29th May 2007.

Snodderly, Beth. 2015. *Shalom: The Goal of the Kingdom and of International*
  Development. Pasadena, CA: William Carey International University Press.

_____. 2015. *Ed. The Goal of International Development: God's Will on Earth,*
  as It Is in Heaven. Pasadena, CA: William Carey International University Press.

Soubbotina, Tatyana P. 2004. *Beyond Economic Growth: An Introduction to Sustainable*
  Development. 2nd ed. Washington D.C.: The World Bank.
    Stanton, Elizabeth A. 2007. "The Human Development Index: A History." *Political*
  Economy Research Institute: University of Massachusetts.

Stearns, Richard. 2014. *The Hole in Our Gospel: What Does God Expect of Us? The*

Answer That Changed My Life and Might Just Change the World. Nashville, TN: Thomas Nelson Inc.

_____. 2014. *Unfinished: Filling the Hole in our Gospel*. Nashville, TN:
Thomas Nelson Inc.

Steger, Manfred B., and Ravi K. Roy. 2010. *Neoliberalism: A Very Short Introduction*.
New York: Oxford University Press Inc.

Stiglitz, Joseph E. 2006. *Making Globalization Work*. New York: W.W. Norton &
Company, Inc.

Swartley, Willard. M. 2012. *Health, Healing and the Church's Mission: Biblical*
Perspectives on Moral Priorities. Downers Grove, Ill: IVP Academic.

Szalavitz, Maia and Bruce D. Perry. 2010. *Born for Love: Why Empathy Is Essential –*
and Endangered. New York: William Morrow.

Szirmai, Adam. 2015. *The Dynamics of Socio-Economic Development*. Cambridge:
Cambridge University Press.

The Chalmers Center. "What is Poverty?" Accessed April 12, 2017.
https://www.chalmers.org/our-work/redefining-poverty/

The Manila Times. 2015. "Only 25% Filipinos financially

literate – S&P." Accessed May

14, 2018 http://www.manilatimes.net/only-25-of-filipinos-financially-literate-sp/232428/

Thorsen, Dag Einar and Amund Lie. 2007. "What is Neoliberalism?" *Department of*
Political Science, University of Oslo.

Tim Allen and Alan Thomas. Eds. 2000. *Poverty and Development: Into the 21st*
Century. 2nd Edition. Oxford, UK: Oxford University Press.

Tipps, Dean C. 1976. "Modernization Theory and the Comparative Study of Societies: a
Critical Perspective." *In Comparative Modernization.*

Tizon, Al. 2008. *Transformation after Lausanne: Radical Evangelical Mission in Global-*
Local Perspective. Oxford, UK: Regnum Books International.

Todd, Scott. 2014. *Hope Rising: How Christians Can End Extreme Poverty in This*
Generation. Tennessee: Thomas Nelson.

Tracy, Steven R. "Common Evangelical Misconceptions of Poverty." Paper presented at
the 63rd annual meetings of the Evangelical Theological Society, San Francisco, CA, November 17, 2011.

Tyndale, Wendy R. Ed. 2006. *Visions of Development: Faith-based Initiatives.*

Burlington, VT: Ashgate.

Ugwueye, Luke Emeka. 2010. "Shalom (שָׁלוֹם)! A Study of the Concept of Peace in the
Old Testament." Pp. 72-75 in *International Journal of Theology & Reformed Tradition*. Vol. 2.

United Nations Development Programme in Philippines. 2016 *Human Development*
Report. New York: United Nations.

United Nations Economic and Social Council. 1998. "Statement of Commitment for
Action to Eradicate Poverty Adopted by Administrative Committee on Coordination." New York: United Nations. Last modified May 20. Accessed October 30, 2017. http://www.un.org/press/en/1998/19980520.eco5759.html

Wafawanaka, Robert. "Is the biblical perspective on poverty that "there shall be no poor
among you" or "you will always have the poor with you"?" *Review and Expositor*, Vol. III (2), 2014.

Walton, Oliver. 2011. "Helpdesk Research Report: Self-esteem, shame and poverty."
Governance and Social Development Resource Center.

Wanak, Lee, ed. 2008. *The Church and Poverty in Asia.* Mandaluyong City, Metro
Manila: OMF Literature Inc.

Ward, Maurice. 2013. "Poverty and Crime." *National Dialogue Network.* Last Modified

October 12. Accessed April 10, 2017. http://www.
nationaldialoguenetwork.org/poverty-and-crime/

Weber, Martin. 2015. "The Meaning of Shalom and the
Spirit of Advent." *Logos Talk.*
    Last Modified December 4. Accessed March 28, 2017.
    https://blog.logos.com/2015/12/the-meaning-of-shalom-
and-the-spirit-of-advent/

Whitham, Graham. 2015. "Measuring poverty in the UK and
why it matters."
    OXFAM. Policy and Practice Blog. Last Modified November
20. Accessed April 5, 2017. http://policy-practice.oxfam.org.
uk/blog/2015/11/measuring-poverty-in-the-uk-and-why-it-
matters

Willard M. Swartley. 2006. *Covenant of Peace.* Grand Rapids,
MI: Eerdmans Publishing
    Co.

Williams, Délice. 2016. "What are the Causes of Poverty?"
The Borgen Project. Last
    Modified June 25. Accessed April 19, 2017.https://
borgenproject.org/what-causes-global-poverty/

Wydick, Bruce. 2015. "Economists Discover Holistic Development." *Across Two*
    Worlds. Last Modified June 29. Accessed October 10, 2017.
http://www.acrosstwoworlds.net/?p=357

Ziai, Aram. 2007. *Exploring Post-development: Theory and practice, problems and*
    perspectives. Abingdon, Oxon: Routledge.

ABOUT THE AUTHOR

Kumar Aryal (PhD, William Carey International University) is professor of intercultural studies at International Graduate School of Leadership. He and his wife, Kathryn, serve with Action International Ministries. Kumar is from Nepal and Kathryn is from the Philippines. They are blessed with two handsome boys, Kevin Daniel and Kyle Joseph Aryal. Currently, they are based in Manila, Philippines.